With best wishes,

Charles de Kunffy

August 30, 1976

CREATIVE HORSEMANSHIP

Charles de Kunffy

SOUTH BRUNSWICK AND NEW YORK:
A. S. BARNES AND COMPANY
LONDON: THOMAS YOSELOFF LTD

A. S. Barnes and Co., Inc.
Cranbury, New Jersey 08512

Thomas Yoseloff Ltd
108 New Bond Street
London W1Y OQX, England

Library of Congress Cataloging in Publication Data

De Kunffy, Charles, 1936—
    Creative horsemanship.

    Bibliography: p.
    1.   Dressage. I. Title.
SF309.5.D44   798'.23   73-10517
ISBN 0-498-01386-3

PRINTED IN THE UNITED STATES OF AMERICA

Contents

Introduction

There seems to be no reason for writing another equestrian book, for there are many outstanding ones already available. In addition to the books written by great theoreticians of the past there are also great contemporary equestrian academicians who are generously active in passing on their superb knowledge to a new generation of expanding equestrian public.

While equestrian literature may seem repetitious, its merits are not diminished. The literature, by its very nature, must be to some extent repetitious. After all, exposing the same principles about the same art form calls for a certain amount of this. Equestrian books are indeed all about the "same story," that is the correct attitude toward horses and the correct techniques and methods for an ideal achievement by horses. However, just as the "story" remains the same in all the pictures painted of the biblical *Last Supper* or the *Crucifixion*, the scores of great painters who painted the same "stories" left us something infinitely valuable by their unique contribution toward a more complete and profound insight into these "stories." Great themes can be restated by great artists in many ways. The more they are restated, the more eloquent the total effect becomes. The more these artistic renderings reiterate the same essential "facts," the easier their comprehension and absorption becomes. Similarly, the seemingly repetitious equestrian literature serves as the invaluable inspiration that causes the true equestrian knowledge and insight.

Before I invite you to read my thoughts on horsemanship, I wish to recommend to you some important books to read. My intentions in writing are to add some further thoughts to the great classics in the already existing literature. I do not wish to restate everything that has been said many times before. My book can be most profitably read IN ADDITION TO already existing texts.

Let me recommend to you a few books in the following pages that I consider absolutely essential reading, prerequisite to becoming a true equestrian. There are many more excellent books than those I recommend. I simply cannot spare the space for them here. Indeed, there should be a recommended bibliography compiled by a good scholar. We could all benefit by one. But that is not my task.

I wish to point out that the order in which I discuss the books I recommend to your attention has no relevance to any order of their importance. There is no attempt on my part for ranking them as to quality. They are all outstanding books, proclaiming the classical principles of horsemanship, all artistically splendid, creative in approach and language.

The Art of Horsemanship, by Xenophon (187 pages), translated, footnoted, and edited by Morris H. Morgan, PhD.; published by J.A. Allen and Co., Ltd., London (1962, 1969).

Xenophon, a Greek general, wrote the oldest existing book on horsemanship. His principles, stated in this book, became the foundation of classical horsemanship and contemporary dressage. The training of horses should be based on understanding rather than compulsion, and the process should involve education rather than conditioning. These were Xenophon's two great principles, still surviving intact in contemporary dressage. The known period of Xenophon's life falls approximately between 401 and 355 B.C. His valuable insight into the nature of the horse is revealed in a highly readable, concise essay. The translator includes samples of the works of other equestrian writers of the Greco-Roman period of antiquity. These writers all continue the tradition Xenophon began.

There are excerpts from Simon, another Greek equestrian; also by the Romans Varro (37 B.C.), Vergil (29 B.C.), Calpurnius Siculus (60 A.D.), *Columella* (65 A D.), Oppion (early third century), Nemesian (late third century), Apsyrtus (early fourth century), Pelagonius (late fourth century), and Palladius (mid fourth century). The variety of topics these equestrians of antiquity deal with is extensive. Their language is most readable, and their advice, to a surprisingly large extent, still valid.

Horse and Man, edited by Luigi Gianoli (442 pages). Published by J.A. Allen and Co., Ltd., London (1969?).

A monumental album with expert articles assessing and exposing the entire contemporary equestrian panorama. This most readable text is enriched by 794 pictures and illustrations, making the book an equestrian spectacle. It is an indispensible vehicle for orientation about the vast variety in contemporary possibilities of equestrian involvement. Its expert articles cover the entire range of activities that involve horses, from harness racing and circus riding to international show jumping competitions and Olympic Dressage riding.

One cannot adequately specialize in dressage without a panoramic concept of horsemanship, which this book presents. No ambitious dressage rider may ignore the fact that he has much to learn that is directly applicable to his art form from others who pursue specialized equestrian interests, other than dressage. Love and respect of the horse are commonly shared attributes of all equestrians, and thus the horse deserves our discovering him in his many roles, talents, and functions. Because a good historical exposition of horsemanship is part of this book, and because its territory of exposure is global, the panorama is all-encompassing.

The Kingdom of the Horse, by H.H. Isenbart and E.M. Buhrer (303 pages). Published by Collins, London and Glasgow (1969?).
Another large album of vast beauty and academic usefulness. Much of what is said about the previous book is applicable to this one also. If you want a one-glance impression of its academic relevance and creative novelty, turn to page 132, and gaze at the "Mathematics of the Manege."

Extensively and beautifully illustrated, this book, as well as the one previously mentioned, can delight any nonequestrian visitor who finds it on the coffee table.

Riding Technique in Pictures, by Lt. Col. C.E.G. Hope and Charles Harris (128 pages). Published by J.A. Allen and Co., Ltd., London (1956, 1960, 1968).
This splendid book shows through 440 photographs and a concise text all those things that verbally cannot be adequately exposed. Indispensable for beginning riders as well as riding instructors, for the book takes pains in explaining all about the riding techniques from mounting a horse to holding the reins of a full bridle. It gives detailed instructions about proper equipment, proper techniques, and proper bodily positions on the horse. Beyond the seemingly tedious trivialities of tack this book offers clear and well-formulated suggestions on exercise sequences for a horse. On pages 40 and 41 there is a clear chart of useful gymnastic exercises for the horse. This outline also includes the purpose of these exercises, and explains the correct aids that the rider must apply to perform them.

While the book is indispensable for precompetition riders and their instructors, it remains a refreshing reminder to sophisticated competition riders and their coaches.

The Complete Training of Horse and Rider, by Alois Podhajsky (287 pages). Published by George G. Harrap and Co., Ltd., London (1965. 1967).

This book fulfills everything its title promises. It is a beautifully written encyclopedic work that scrupulously follows the principles of classical horsemanship to which its author has outstandingly dedicated his life.

It is not an easily digestible book for beginners and those not well acquainted with equestrian theory. It is, however, the standard expertise for other experts. However, any serious rider, even novices, should read it from cover to cover, just to be stunned by the prospects and possibilities of future involvement in the art of dressage. Indeed, the humility gained by not understanding all that is exposed in this book, may serve as a valuable character-building experience to the less initiated.

The author is not only one of the greatest equestrian academicians of all times, but a man of vast practical experience in the training of dressage horses and riders. This book is both the alphabet and the dictionary of classical horsemanship.

Dressage Riding, by Richard Watjen (113 pages). Published by J.A. Allen and Co., Ltd., London (1958, 1961, 1965).

An exquisitely clear, well-organized exposition of both elementary dressage and *haute école* by a great master. It is once more an encyclopedic text, but due to its outstanding organization and explicitness the complex topic is rendered relatively easy for assimilation.

The Finer Points of Riding, by A.K. Frederiksen (85 pages). Published by J.A. Allen and Co., Ltd., London (1969).

This brief, concise, clear, and informative book is the right response to the burning need for an easily digestible handbook on dressage.

Because the book is a lucid condensation of vast knowledge of the classical dressage principles, it strikes the reader with an almost poetic impact. Stingy with words to the point of a telegram, yet it manages to do justice to its topic. It should be read like a poem, in one sitting, to really savor its bravura, and then gone back to periodically for looking up specifics as the need may arise.

The book's determination to "not do it all" again in encyclopedic depth and width, makes it ever so much the very book that was so missed and asked for before its publication. This is a book one should "have around" on night stands, in glove compartments, and in instructional rooms of equestrian centers.

Rules for Dressage Competitions, by the Federation Equestre Internationale (43 pages). Published by the Federation Equestre Internationale, Avenue Hamoir 38, Bruxelles 18, Belgium.

This booklet, republished yearly, represents the final authority's view on dressage and competition of dressage. Not only is the word *dressage* defined in this booklet, but so are all the paces and movements used in international dressage competitions. The booklet includes all international dressage competition rules as well as regulations concerning the competition size dressage court and its distances from judges, riders, and the public. This booklet is not only indispensable to international competitors, but to any equestrian in need of definitions of terminology, to anyone planning to construct a proper dressage court, and to others who may judge dressage shows.

The Olympic Dressage Test in Pictures, by Gregor de Romaszkan (143 pages). Published by Pelham Books Ltd., London (1968).

A superb, pictorial participation in the riding of the Olympic Grand Prix de Dressage test (highest level of competition dressage test). For all horsemen a visual thrill, for those with dressage competition ambitions an acquaintance with their ultimate goal, and for those who are doing it, a fine review.

As far as the Olympic Grand Prix de Dressage test is concerned, all is there, both pictorially and verbally. With a little imagination one can ride right along. One must always have the ultimate goal in mind in order to succeed. Acquaintance with it can never be soon enough.

Give Your Horse a Chance, by Lt. Col. A.L. d'Endrody (543 pages). Published by J.A. Allen and Co., Ltd., London (1959, 1967).

This is the great book on three-day-event riding and showing jumping. As dressage in part and parcel to correct cross-country riding and stadium jumping, it is, of course, a book on dressage. This book is all-inclusive and thorough on its subject. So wide is its spectrum that it includes instructions on how to build courses, how to warm up for competitions, and how to chisel and polish a dressage test, even while riding in front of the judges. It is a pragmatic book, scrupulously practical, yet endlessly gushing with new ideas. It is the work of an obviously creative mind, the kind of masterpiece that will not easily have a peer.

It is the most comprehensive work on jumping, and all in complete accordance with the classical equestrian principles of dressage.

Cavalletti, by Reiner Klimke (128 pages). Published by J.A. Allen and Co., Ltd., London (1960).

Superbly illustrated with photos, drawings, and diagrams, this is a remarkable handbook on Cavalletti work. Cavalletti is a most important form of exercise in classical riding, not only for jumpers, but even for horses specializing in dressage. Cavalletti, if not a medicine for all ills, is certainly medication for most ills, and serves so many useful purposes that I must recommend its extensive application.

Dr. Klimke is an active competitor, one of the greatest contemporary riders, participator in Olympic games, world championships, and other international events. He demonstrates in this book his versatile academic knowledge, and his great facility in using a most readable pen.

My Horses, My Teachers, by Alois Podhajsky (202 pages). Published by George G. Harrap and Co., Ltd., London (1967, 1968, 1969, 1970).

A great tribute to many great riding instructors, the horses who taught most to one of the greatest equestrians of all time. An autobiographical account of a lifetime spent dedicated to horses. The reader will meet not only great horse-instructors, but also one of the greatest human pupils horses ever had. The excellent style of this book elevates it to great literature. No reader can escape a transformation of his attitude toward horses, and I can imagine this book to transform a "mere rider" into a true horseman.

Horse Psychology, by Moyra Williams (191 pages). Published by Methuen Co., Ltd., London (1956).

The list of recommended reading would be quite incomplete without calling to your attention this good book on animal nature in general, and the nature of the horse in particular. No one can attain horsemanship without profound insight into the nature of the horse, which is the center of the horseman's concern.

In a mechanized and urbanized age, where most equestrians live in complete lack of intimacy with, and proximity to, nature, the horse may well become an unnaturally mysterious natural phenomenon. To avoid this, one must turn to books in order to bridge the gap between our urbanized self and the horse, that natural ancient companion.

Know Your Horse, by Lt. Col. W.S. Codrington (186 pages). Published by J.A. Allen and Co., Ltd., London (1955, 1963, 1966, 1968).

A most informative book concerning the health and care of the horse. Detecting and treating diseases and injuries, correct shoeing, management of bad habits, are all discussed in this book. All equestrians owe it to themselves and their horse to know all that is written here, even if they insist on the best veterinary, blacksmith, and groom attention for their horses. There is no equestrian success without knowing about grooming, diet, shoeing, and general health of the horse.

Creative Horsemanship

1
The Nature of the Ideal Horseman

A horseman is identifiable by his outstanding concern for the well-being of horses in general, and for his horses in particular. My writing is relevant to those horsemen who are interested in riding according to classical principles of dressage. These horsemen will inevitably be sportsmen, and if they grow to be outstanding, they might become artists.

I believe that all sports improve the participants' bodies. They all sharpen the awareness of sportsmen's senses. Furthermore, sports enable people to control and coordinate the actions of their bodies. Sports inevitably affect the sportsman's mental attitude and personal characteristics. Therefore, in general, they serve to improve people both physically and mentally.

Few sports improve people as much as riding does. Few sports demand as total a physical and mental involvement as riding. Like all other sports, riding also demands a great deal of inborn talent or aptitude. Certain physical characteristics are desirable, while certain mental characteristics are indispensable.

Physically, the ideal rider should have a height between about five feet four inches and six feet, and be slender and well proportioned. Ideally, the rider's legs will be long, proportionately to the upper body, and slender in the thighs. The ideal rider will have an erect carriage, and attractive coordination in movement. He will be physically supple and quite enduring. He will be strong, but not robust.

The attitude of an equestrian must change and grow to include patience, humility, tolerance, optimism, consistency, and empathy with the horse. Good prospects for horsemanship incorporate these attitudes to some degree in their nature, but it must be stressed that these attitudes can always be furthered, improved, and encouraged. Without them no outstanding achievement is possible in riding, which is a character-improving art form.

15

Horsemanship is based on the love of the horse. These attitudes develop early. These two California girls are becoming equestrians.

By observation, one can easily support the generalization that most great equestrian, those who consistently achieve outstanding results in competition, also have a great sense of humor. Obviously, a sense of humor does not affect horses directly. They will not listen to our jokes and witticisms and have a good laugh periodically. But a person with a good sense of humor is one who possesses a typically optimistic outlook, a good sense of proportion in life, exuberance toward work, courage and daring, and usually an ample capacity to love. With a good sense of humor one can admit mistakes, tolerate temporary failures, and consider setbacks as educational experiences rather than as encouragements for contemplating suicide. In short, humor is symptomatic of attitudes that are important for equestrians, rather than being a direct asset in riding.

Certain characteristics must be cultivated in equestrians. They must increase the speed of their reactions. They must be able to concentrate deeply and for a long time. They must increase awareness of their en-

Elegant not only in attire but in demeanor, concentration, and carriage, the rider displays the passage, the most elegant of all movements. Pomp and splendor are brought to mind with this elevated, slow-motion trot that seems to be floating above the ground without touching it. Mrs. Kyra Downton is on Kadet.

The magnificent beauty of the horse is the lure, his great energy is the thrill, his attention is the challenge, and his kindness is the reward of horse-manship. Condus, the Trakhener stud, at his home in Iserlohn, Germany.

vironment, and increase their awareness of the horse's movements.

Riders should present an air of formality, a most becoming compliment to the equestrian tradition, which represents an elegant sport and an art form of exquisite beauty. Elegance is far from being merely a composed, harmonious exterior, though that is indispensable for properly wearing a formal riding attire. Elegance is also an inner posture that has to do with unfailing loyalty, trust-worthiness, a sense of justice toward the horse, oneself, the instructor, judge, and the entire art form. Elegance is revealed by a sense of perseverance to know, which remains restlessly disatisfied with anything short of perfection. Elegance is always obvious through a sense of humility toward the horse and oneself; a sense of honor that precludes abuse of the horse and invites consistent fair play.

Physical and mental elegance is best displayed by an attitude of concentration. A concentrated man is never self-conscious, for he is preoccupied by something other than himself. He has combined self-awareness, knowledge of personal worth, and relaxation into a physical and inner posture that never fails to connote elegance.

2
Horsemanship

I intend to use the term *horsemanship* to denote a specific human attitude toward horses. This attitude is eminently characterized by concern for the well-being of the horse. Consequently, a horseman, or an *equestrian*, is not just anybody interested in or involved with horses. Horsemen are different from others because they will demonstrate their love for horses by adhering to the *classical principles* of horse training. These classical principles have a more than two-thousand-year-old tradition, a tradition that is based on the philosophy that horses respond to kindness, that they are educable and with patient, gradual education will display their natural abilities to the highest degree. Training of horses should be based on gradual and natural educational methods. All horse training or education that is based on this classical philosophy is now called *dressage* (even if its goal may be jumping or trail riding).

Since classical horsemanship is a rather ancient art form, much theoretical knowledge has been accumulated about it and has been bequeathed to us. The effectiveness of these theoretical principles of classical horsemanship has been amply demonstrated throughout many centuries. These principles, and only these, continue to yield the outstanding results of contemporary international equestrian competitions, including those of the Olympic games and the Equestrian World Championships. Only those riders succeed consistently in contemporary international equestrian events who are true horsemen, adhering to the principles of classical riding.

There can be no success in horsemanship without extensive theoretical knowledge. This can best be acquired by reading as much as possible the extensive literature on the subject. While reading is prerequisite to becoming an equestrian, it should also be supplemented by discussions with knowledgeable equestrians, experts and authorities on classical

Mrs. Kyra Downton with her late Olympic horse Kadet, at her home in Atherton, California. An equestrian finds pleasure in the company of her horse. Far beyond riding extends the bond between horse and rider as they share many times of affection, relaxation, and communication.

horsemanship. Attendance of lectures, discussions, and viewing of equestrian films are of utmost importance for a horseman's education.

Needless to say, actual riding, according to the learned classical principles, is the most important educational device. After all, one learns equestrian theory in order to apply it every day in practice.

3
Dressage: The Classical Form of Riding

The word *dressage* is now well understood by many equestrians, and an increasing number of these equestrians are now riding their horses according to classical dressage principles. Dressage riding finds its origins in the writings of the ancient Greek general Xenophon, and is based on a two-thousand-year-old tradition of horsemanship. During these two thousand years everything has been tried, and that which succeeded in improving a horse was retained. This practical, effective way of riding, based on two thousand years of accumulated knowledge, has been handed down to us as the classical riding heritage.

Because horses were, in the past, the most useful of men's partners, the knowledge of horses and their effective training has been an all-important aspect of human existence. Horses were beasts of burden, extensions and enlargement of men's muscles and energies. They were the fastest means of transportation, both civilian and military, making them as important in the past as are jets in our day. As a consequence of their importance, which endured for so many millennia, men spent much time to crystallize their knowledge of the horse. Only in most recent times, and then only in mechanized societies, has the utilitarian value of the horse declined. However, concurrently their value as sport partner has increased, as men have found themselves reluctant to leave contact with nature, and abandon such a fine partner in pleasure and work as the horse. No tradition that has developed for millennia can be easily discarded in two generations.

Dressage has three basic, interrelated meanings:

1. Dressage in general is all horsemanship that is based on love and respect for horses. When we use the concept of dressage in this conno-

tation, we often call it gymnasticizing. The perpetual, reasonable, well-planned, systematic gymnasticizing of the horse will result in a development similar to that occurring in human gymnasts, or figure skaters, or ballet dancers: while their muscles and joints are improving in strength, and their ability to use this strength or increased energy, with control, also improves, they become supple. A supple body manifests itself in harmonious, controlled, well-coordinated use of an extremely strong, well-developed musculature. It enables the body to dispense a great deal of energy with comfort and without stress. It is aimed at the improvement of the horse's natural abilities to the ultimate degree. It results in a happy horse that usually lives longer, stays healthier, and performs better and for a longer time than one not trained according to dressage principles. The method of dressage includes only natural means for the development of the horse. It is based on commitment to the education of the horse. Therefore, it is based on mutual understanding, respect,

Roderick Johnson on a green horse at the ordinary canter. The horse is on the forehand but relaxed, even, and on the aids. This is the foundation from which the movement can be improved.

and trust between horse and rider. It is based on kindness and rewards rather than punishment. It excludes the use of force and intimidation.

2.   Dressage, more specifically, refers to the logical, natural, sequential exercising of the horse, in order to improve his natural physical and mental abilities. It makes possible a maximum performance output with a minimum of energy dispensation. As the right joints and correct musculature are being used for the performance of a task, exhaustion is eradicated, and stress, both physical and mental, is reduced.

As all education, dressage is based on clear and consistent communication. When the rider communicates to his horse, he uses aids that are usually bodily attitudes rather than words. The horse also constantly communicates to his rider with his body. The horse's communications must be understood clearly by the rider, who must have a "listening ability" to these, which we call "feel."

3.   Dressage, finally, also denotes a special kind of competition. Essentially, dressage competitions are formalized gymnasticizing. This

Mrs. Kyra Downton, Pan-American Games Gold winner, United States Olympic participant, veteran of international dressage competitions, showing her Olympic horse, the Holstein-Arabian Kadet, at Pebble Beach, California. Beyond a polished display of all the accomplishments of a classically trained horse, dressage competitions should be memorable for their aesthetic value. The horse-rider artistic unit is showing in magnificent natural surroundings that enhance the aesthetic value of his competition.

type of competition is simply based on showing a horse in a flat arena of prescribed size, in which the horse is ridden through logical gymnastic exercises that are prescribed in a specific program. Dressage competition is based on valuable daily gymnastic exercises, the only difference being that these gymnastics are being performed in a prescribed area and proceed according to a well-designed, logical program. Depending on the horse's gymnastic advancement, he can be shown on different levels of gymnastics. The program is logically put together, asking for a logical sequence of exercises that can best display the horse's athletic achievements within a short period of time.

The horses that are being shown in dressge competitions have been trained according to the dressage principles of the classical riding tradition. The daily gymnastic dressage exercises of a horse should aim at the following goals:

Physically, the horse should be strengthened and balanced in order to increase his impulsion, and as a result be able to carry himself and his rider straight forward. In order to do that the horse must improve his suppleness (ability to bend), move evenly, and in clear rhythm in all natural paces. He must become elastic in the controlled use of his body.

Mentally, the horse should become obedient to his rider as a result of trust that is based on cooperation and consistent communication of guidance and suggestion. The rider must represent reason, logic, and kindness, much like our thinking ought to represent these attributes to the rest of our organism, which willingly obeys its dictates. The horse must also improve his attentiveness. Without an increased attention span, as well as an improved sensitivity of awareness, a horse cannot accommodate the ever-refined communication of the rider's aids, nor can he improve his facility in self-awareness and resultant coordination.

The horse's physical and mental development (1) are taking place simultaneously, (2) are reinforcing each other, and (3) are achieved by systematic, logical, and consistent gymnastic exercises. These gymnastic exercises include basically two kinds: exercises that a) longitudinally bend (reflex) the horse, or exercises that b) laterally bend the horse.

Longitudinal bending of the horse refers to the horse's flexion throughout his length. As the horse creates all his locomotion with his hindquarters, yet has most of his bulk in front of these hindquarters, he cannot easily propel himself forward without the total engagement of his body. In order to totally engage he has to correctly flex his muscles throughout his body, which results in longitudinal bending. This bending begins with locomotion (energy, impulse to move) at the hind hoofs, run

Mrs. Kyra Downton on Kadet at the collected trot and working trot.

The longitudinal bending of a free horse: Condus, Trakhener stallion.

Mrs. Kyra Downton on Kadet in passage: the horse is so well engaged, croup lowered, that he seems to be going up a hill, rising at his forehand.

through the joints of the hindlegs and quarters. The locomotive energy (impulsion) is communicated through the back muscles to the front, where the impulsion is fed into the supporting shoulder and forehand area and the navigational (balancing) areas of neck and head. The impulsive energy finally terminates at the horse's mouth.

The results of longitudinal flexion are well-engaged joints and a relaxed but active musculature. Both of these contribute in general to the creation of great impulsive energy that can be controlled, maintained, and contained by the rider. Specifically it results in an improved ability of the horse to (1) carry the rider in correct balance (the composite weight of rider and horse being evenly distributed over his legs), (2) shift the center of gravity of the composite weight toward the hindquarters, which are the only source of locomotion (making movement more effortless), (3) increase the horse's ability of collection and extension (the horse's ability to lengthen or shorten his strides in all natural paces without altering the rhythm of his hoof beats. In other words, the horse will cover greater or shorter distances per unit of time without either rushing or slowing down.

Here is shown a green horse still moving on the forehand, yet beginning to balance by virtue of longitudinal bending. Rhythm, relaxation, and acceptance of aids, including the bit, are established. From this base, by driving the hindlegs deeper under the rider's seat and gymnasticizing the horse to enable him to lower the haunches, he will eventually be able to shift more weight into the hindquarters.

The ideal working trot performed by Hilda Gurney on Keen: straight, longitudinally well-bent, engaged hindquarters, lowering of the croup, elastic and ample impulsion, a swinging back, obedience, attention, and relaxation.

Roderick Johnson of Las Vegas, Nevada on his late horse Nuget at the collected trot. As a teenager Roderick rode Western-horse-turned-dressage-horse Nuget to many successes. There was relaxation, rhythm, elasticity, engagement, bending of the haunches, and total harmony as great achievements resulting from correct dressage work. Yet the tall and slender rider always looked aesthetically hindered by his small, stocky mount. Dressage, an art presenting beauty, expects that the rider select a horse properly suited to his own conformation in order to reach the top in competition.

Balanced movement is one of the foundations of all great riding achievements. The other is the rider's ability to control the horse's hindquarters, which are the source of his impulsion and forward energies. Both the horse's balance and the rider's control of his "engine" can only occur as a result of longitudinal flexion of the horse. Without that there cannot be relaxation of musculature, elasticity of the joints, and therefore no control over the activities of his hindquarters.

All four photographs show the extended trot. Dressage gymnasticizing will result in the ability of the horse to extend or collect his strides as well as his entire body without losing the original rhythm of the strides. This variation from a long and flat moving to a short, but high-moving horse proves utmost elasticity of joints and muscles. The ultimate goal of dressage is a straight horse eager to move forward. These extended trot pictures show that in order to do so the horse must engage with the hindquarters, lower his croup, and stride with the hind hooves past the hoof prints of the forelegs. The horses under saddle are longitudinally bent to carry correctly, in balance, the riders weight above with weight following from behind.

The best exercises for improving longitudinal flexion are transitions. It is important to know that transitions can not only take place from pace to pace (trot to walk), but also within paces by extending (lengthening) or collecting (shortening) the horse's strides.

Mrs. Kyra Downton competing at Pebble Beach, California on the Thoroughbred Crescendo. Both photographs are at passage. The one on the left is on a circle, therefore representing a high degree of longitudinal collection, simultaneously shown through lateral bending. The right shows passage on a center line with only longitudinal engagement.

The most collected gymnastic exercises are the collected walk, the piaffe (trot on the spot), and the pirouette at the canter.

Pirouette at the canter, performed by Mrs. Kyra Downton on Kadet.

Lateral bending (flexion) refers to the horse's ability to bend from side to side. When a horse is correctly bent he will stay in balance while supporting the weight he carries through turns. This kind of bending, which insures that the horse remains balanced through turns without compromising any of his forward impulsion, will occur only when the horse is evenly bent throughout the length of his spinal column.

The lateral bending of a free horse: Condus volunteering the shoulder in on a circle.

Obviously, less supple horses with relatively little gymnastic background will be less able to bend on an arc than a thoroughly elastic, well gymnasticized horse. Therefore, riders must be careful not to over-bend one part of the novice horse's body only, for that will invite him to remain straight and stiff in the rest of his body. Obviously, the horse's neck is naturally more supple than his bulky trunk, which includes a relatively unyielding ribcage and heavy musculature. A horse can remain rigid throughout his trunk, and still bend the neck to reach a fly or scratch himself far back.

Miss Hilda Gurney on Keen performing the volte at the collected canter.
This is the smallest circle performed, its diameter being the length of the
horse. Throughout this exercise the keenest lateral bending is shown on
any single-track movement. An excellent example.

As stated before, correct lateral bending occurs only when the horse is evenly bent throughout his body, along his spinal column. Most of the time a horse is required to move on a bent line (arc). Only seldom will a rider offer a straight path to move on. In our small riding arenas there are two long walls and two short walls where a horse should move straight. Otherwise riding is done on arcs, circles, or the combinations of those, whether it is jumping or other gymnastic exercises the rider may pursue.

Generalizations to remember in connection with lateral bending of the horse:

1. Longitudinal bending is always a prerequisite (condition to any lateral bending. In other words, lateral bending can occur only when a horse is "ahead of the boots, driven up to the bit," in perfect longitudinal flexion, responding to the aids.

2. While lateral bending exercises can never be done with a straight

Lateral bending through corners at the canter, performed by Mrs. Kyra Downton.

horse, their purpose remains to help straighten a horse. Lateral bending exercises have a very high suppling value that insures the eventual development of the desired straight-moving horse.

3. During all lateral bending exercises horses are bent evenly in the entire length of their spinal columns toward one side. That side is the hollow, or contracted side of the horse, and called his "inside," regardless of whether it is toward the center or the rail of the arena. The other side, called the "outside," is longer, and feels full.

4. While longitudinal flexion is prerequisite to lateral flexion, one reinforces the horse's ability to do the other. In other words, each successful lateral bending will consolidate the horse's ability to remain in longitudinal bending which, in turn, makes this prerequisite position more consistently available to do additional lateral exercises.

5. Always perform each lateral bending exercise on both hands. Never exercise the horse's "hollow side" or "stiff side" more than the other. Always "mirror" lateral exercises, and do it right away. (If you circle to the right, follow it soon with a circle to the left. If you make a half-pass to the right, follow it with one done to the left, etc.)

6. Always combine longitudinal and lateral gymnastics. Longitudinal gymnastics, being all transitions, always make a transition after each lateral exercise. (Circle right in the trot, and reaching the rail depart into canter. Or half-pass to the right in the trot, and reaching the opposite rail, depart into canter on the left lead. Or pirouette at the walk, and depart at the canter on right lead when pirouette is completed.) The combinations are literally infinite.

7. Gymnastic riding can be only meaningful when planned strategy is pursued by the rider. No exercises should be done on the spur of the moment and without due preparation. During riding, but not abruptly, quick succession of changes reveal well planned gymnasticizing. There is no specific value in riding endlessly in the same pace, on the same line, for a long time. The frequency of transitions is in direct proportion with the value of gymnastic development to the horse.

Lateral bending can be exercised in two qualitatively different ways:

1. The more simple lateral exercises are those done on circular lines. In such instances, the horse's hindlegs continue to follow toward the direction of the forelegs (similar to proceeding on straight lines) on the corresponding side. Such lateral movements include all the corners of a riding arena, those being all parts of an incomplete circle. To that we can add the riding of a full circle, which can be of any size. It should be large for a stiffer, novice horse, and smaller according to the horse's ability to bend as he advances in his sup-

pleness. Then we can ride serpentine lines, which are more difficult than simple circles, for the horse is asked to bend and redistribute his center of gravity from side to side in quick succession. Finally, we can ride figure eights, which are rather difficult to do well, because the horse will have to sustain bending for a long while on each side, yet is given one straight step to change his bending and center of gravity from one side to the other.

In short, from simple to complex arc riding we proceed from an arc, through the circle and serpentine, to the figure eight. We also proceed from generous arcs to tighter, smaller ones, as the horse's ability to bend into them in a continuum improves.

2.   The more difficult or complex lateral exercises are done on multi-tracks. That means that the horse will not follow with his hindlegs toward the direction of the forelegs on the corresponding side. Rather, the horse will leave either three or four tracks behind—printed by his hoofs in the sand. These exercises, in their general order of difficulty, are as follows:

The *shoulder-in and shoulder-out* exercises can be done only at the walk and at the trot. In the shoulder-in exercises we ask the horse to be bent around our inside leg, stepping with his inside hindleg toward the footprint of the outside foreleg. He will leave three tracks behind as a result, and will bend generously the inside hindleg by striding deeply under the center of gravity. As a result his shoulder will move somewhat inside the rail. While the horse will progress in space toward the direction of his outside shoulder, he will be bent in the opposite direction of progression, to the inside. This is the only movement we ask of a horse where we demand bending opposite from the direction of progression.

The shoulder-out is the reverse of the shoulder-in. It is advisable to do it, inspite of the fact that by changing hand one can supple equally both sides of the horse with the shoulder-in alone. The shoulder-out supples, and therefore collects, the horse move successfully on advanced levels of training.

The *rump in and rump-out* exercises are a little more sophisticated in their demands on the horse's musculature and joints than the previously discussed ones. In the rump-in (traverse) the horse is once more bent evenly along his spinal column around the rider's inside leg. He is moving his hindquarters toward the side on which he is bent, tracking inside the rail on which the forehands proceed. The outside hindleg of the horse strides toward the direction of his inside foreleg.

The rump-in can be done in all three natural paces, the walk, trot, and canter. However, I strongly recommend never to exercise it in the canter. Horses have the natural tendency to canter crookedly, with their

The shoulder-in is the simplest two-track lateral movement. Here Mrs. Patricia Sullivan performs on Doncaster shoulder-in to the left and to the right at the trot.

Shoulder-in to the left, by Miss Hilda Gurney of Woodland Hills, California, on Witukind, a Hanoverian.

rumps in. That is highly undesirable, for it allows the horse to avoid bending his joints correctly and move out of balance. Indeed, the rider must encourage his horse to canter very straight. Thus, the rump-in at the canter, while horses are eager to offer it, should be avoided as an exercise.

Half pass to the left at trot, performed by Mrs. Kyra Downton on Kadet.

The rump-out (Revers) is the same exercise in reverse bending.

The *half-pass* is a more sophisticated lateral bending exercise than either of the previously described ones. During the half-pass the horse is once again bent around the inside leg of the rider, proceeding toward the direction of his bending. The horse must remain in a position generally parallel to the rail from which it moved away, proceeding sideways toward the opposite rail, where he will be straightened and moved on the opposite hand. Half-passes can be done at the walk, trot, and canter, and should be done,indeed, at all three paces. The horse moving in half-pass will leave four tracks behind on the ground.

Pirouettes are also lateral bending exercises. They can be performed only in the walk and in the canter. While pirouetting at the walk is a relatively simple gymnastic exercise, doing the same at the canter is one of the most difficult. Green horses can soon pirouette at the walk, but only the most advanced horses will be able to do the same at the canter, usually several years later.

At the pirouette the horse is asked to turn around his inside hindleg, which are to remain active, but on the spot where the movement was started. One can ride quarter, half, three-quarter, or full pirouettes, depending on the horse's level of advancement. During these turns around the hindquarters the horse has to be gently bent around the rider's inside leg toward the direction of the turn.

4
Education of the Dressage Rider

The Dressage rider goes through basically three stages of education and achievement:

    1.   The *beginner* should ideally have two instructors, one being the

Young beginner rider learning to harmonize with horse, working toward an independent seat without which there is no horsemanship, at the Hannoversche Reit- und Fahrschule at Verden/Aller.

riding coach, and the other a school horse. The rider is the sole object of instruction. At the beginning, the rider is to learn to harmonize with all the movements of his horse. In order to do so he must acquire a balanced seat that will enable him to follow the horse's movements. A school horse can offer quiet tolerance and well-balanced, comfortable, sure movements without much need of driving by the rider. Thus, the rider can relax into a comfortable position. Lazy horses that need strenuous driving will always stiffen the novice rider. Unbalanced, irregular, unpredictably behaving horses will deny good feeling to the rider, and will cause anguish, anticipation, and loss of courage in him.

This epoch of riding is terminated, depending on the rider's natural talents, as soon as he acquires an independent, balanced seat in which he can follow all of his horse's movements.

2.   In the second stage the rider learns the *craftsmanship* and *technique* of riding. Essential to this development is *diversification* and *building of routine*. During this stage the rider is taught by the coach and continues to learn from his horse. However, he himself becomes to some degree an instructor of his horse. As a consequence, both the rider and the horse become objects of instruction. To help diversify the rider's experience he should ride as many kinds of horses as possible. He should ride in as many modes of riding as possible (trail rides, jumping, flat work, etc.).

The diversification of horse and rider may go concurrently as they take cross-country rides. Nothing will benefit the horse better than rides over open country. The horse becomes attentive, develops impulsion, and has a zestful forward urge. He will valance over uneven terrain and encounter natural obstacles for jumping. The rider's balance, alertness, and courage improve. Without cross-country riding, no horse can gain the physical strength and balance necessary for dressage and jumping. These longeing pictures were taken as Singing Hill riding school, El Cajon, California, where horses and riders work according to the classical equestrian traditions.

The rider also has to learn the refined language of aids, and how to use them effectively and consistently. Now having an independent seat, he can take the liberty to use any part of his body according to need separately, or harmoniously coordinated, without the urgency to grip or stiffen. Learning the use of aids also depends on natural talent. Some people will use effective aids consistently rather soon.

3.   In the third stage the rider is *accomplished*. Now he only needs a coach to guide him and do as much of that work through consultations and discussions as possible. The rider now is his horse's teacher. The horse emerges as the sole object of instruction for which the rider and his coach pool their knowledge and energies.

Some riders will exhibit only great skill and craftmanship in teaching their horses. They will improve throughout a lifetime as experience and routine increase their effectiveness. Others, however, may emerge as artists. Through sensitivity, talent, imagination, and creative approaches they may add to the great body of classical riding knowledge their new inspirations.

At this accomplished stage riding is full of challenges. Competition serves as educational experience. Riders pit themselves against their own performances, and seek to improve. They are now totally dedicated to their horses, having no more need to concentrate on their own skills.

For accomplished riders independence is important. They must exercise their own judgment, and base it on their feeling on the horse. No authoritarian or tyrannical coaching has any place in this experience, for such would limit the rider's development through insight.

The craftsmanship and technique of riding are based on correct *communication between horse and rider*. Communication must always be both ways. One cannot be an effective rider unless one (1) feels clearly and distinctly the communications of his horse, and (2) can interpret them in order to (3) react to them properly. Horses, just like the rider who takes his cues from them, will communicate through bodily attitudes. Riders will feel these communications likewise with their bodies, and reply to them bodily. The language of the rider is called *aids*, and the speech that communicates with the horse is called *aiding*.

The most important general concept in aiding is that AT ALL TIMES ALL THE AIDING MECHANISMS SHOULD BE USED, AND IN PERFECT COORDINATION with each other; that aiding is PERPETUAL, and that the aids must be used CONSISTENTLY.

When thinking of aiding, most horsemen immediately think of dealing with "hands, seat, and boots." Well, not quite. Let me clarify my position.

Rider Roderick Johnson on Saddlebred mare Miss Millionaire from Las Vegas, Nevada, competing at Pebble Beach, California, successfully in a three-day event.

In dressage test on first day.

Weighing in before cross-country ride, second day.

Trotting on roads and trail during cross-country phase.

Galloping with a tired but courageous, willing, and attentive horse toward the finish line after having jumped the strenuous course.

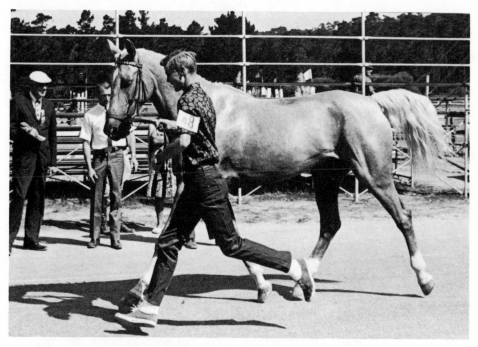

Rider trots along with his horse during veterinary examination on third day, prior to stadium jumping.

Stadium jumping includes a bank.

The water jump.

A rider should basically ride with his upper body, whose actions are communicated through the seat to the horse. Only in coordination with the rider's torso, and in support of its actions can we meaningfully work with our legs and hands. The rider's body is mistakenly called *seat*. However, a good rider merely sits on three points adhesively all the time, and never allows those to leave the horse. These three points are the two seat bones and the crotch. If the crotch is not on the saddle, but elevated off it, the seat bones also rise up into the buttocks, and meaninglessly roll back and forth in the saddle. This annuls any reasonable transfer of communications the body is to transmit to the horse through seat contact. So the seat (the two seat bones and the crotch) is to be a passive, adhesive, and everlastingly contacting communication area in the saddle. Against that seat, then, the aiding system may be put to work. Only in jumping seat (which includes posting) will this seat be replaced by another area of contact and suspension, that of the rider's knees and thighs against which the aids will work.

The flying changes of lead at the canter. All performed by Mrs. Kyra Downton. The horse must remain straight while changing his leads, and must do it in tempo and with ample, long strides.

Now let me outline the four specific instruments of aiding:

1. The *seat*, as described above, is passive, and is the communication center. There rider and horse, through the saddle, fuse in steady contact. This is the area that NEVER aids, but without which there is no possibility of effective aiding elsewhere. This is the point of stability and suspension that allows for the independent mobility of aiding areas.

2. The *boots* are the rider's legs, so called to avoid confusion with the horse's legs. Primarily, the boots mobilize the horse. They serve primarily the purpose of creating impulsion. Impulsion is the most important output we want from the horse. Secondly, the boots are used for the regulating of impulsion into lengthening or higher (more cadenced) and therefore shorter strides. In other words, they regulate extension and collection. They determine paces by their various usage, indicating to the horse both the pace in which he is to move, and the length of strides in that pace. Thirdly, boots also bend the horse, and displace the shoulders or hindquarters when needed.

3. The *body* of the rider is used as a transformer. The impulsion generated in the horse's hindquarters runs forward in his body through his back. These various weave movements (heaving) in the horse's back are absorbed into the rider's supple body. The

Kathy Alles of San Diego, California demonstrates the balanced halt with the rider immobile yet relaxed and ready to apply any aid invisibly.

Correct, harmonious, independent, relaxed seat with all aids working invisibly and close to the horse. Refined aids "whisper" rather than "shout" at the horse from a distance. Closeness of legs, deep seat, and fine hands can aid always on time and not out of rhythm. This harmonious intimacy of aids insures correct results, for it is never how much and how strong the aid is, but rather how well it is timed and refined that yields the best results.

The rider's lower arms, wrists, hands, and the reins must be in a straight continuation connecting the rider's elbows to the horse's mouth. The elbows are part of the rider's back and must stabilize the hands. The wrists and fingers may invite or yield, and the relaxed lower arms may move slightly up or down or from side to side without changing the elbow's restful, steady position. The thumb stands up in pressing against the fore-finger to apply enough pressure for unaltered rein contact. Only the pressure of the thumb can be applied without introducing any stiffness in the arm muscles. The arms and hands, by pointing toward the horse's mouth in a straight line, must have a forward expression, ready to yield by feeding the rein into the impulsively moving horse's mouth.

Even during this restraining invitation with the hands, they continue to look forward, ready to yield.

The yielding hand: the most important instrument of the rider, revealing the most important attitude of the classical rider—forward urge, suppleness, kindness, gentle contact for communication, absorbtion of movement.

These two photographs show the correct leg position of the rider. The position as well as the relaxation of the thighs, yet with a string calf, are achieved by a deep-knee position, legs hanging perpendicularly under the rider's seat and with a well-flexed heel. Without a keen flexion of the heel and supply absorbent ankles, this position cannot be maintained. Stirrups close to the rows help form a longer foot, the only kind that can sink the heel deep.

Legs seen from behind and front, demonstrating that the well-placed legs never leave the horse's sides. Rather they work with and into the horse's side muscles with enough relaxation so as not to produce pain.

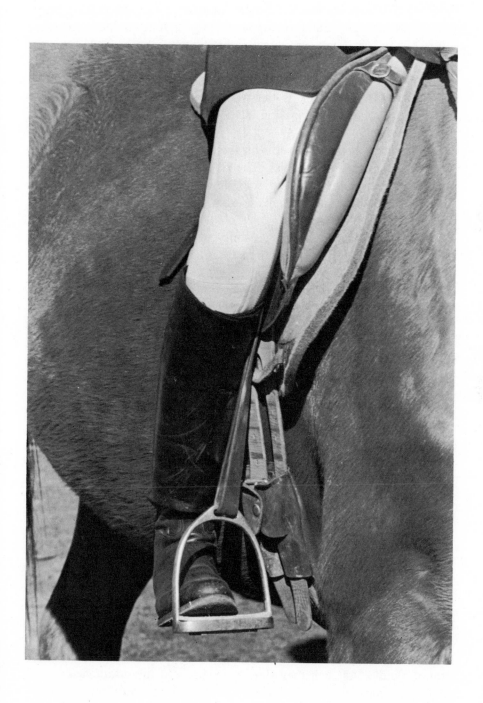

rider perceives these waves and variedly cooperates with them in order to keep his seat steady in the saddle. Without these motion weaves we would sit on an unmoving surface, much like the seat of a car that gives us no feeling in spite of the locomotion of the car. The horse, through his swinging back, feeds the rider his impulsion-created energies. The horse's front never creates locomotive energies, merely absorbs those coming from the hindquarters. The back is the bridge that transports these energies from points of origination in the rear to points of termination in the front.

The rider's body sits on this bridge of communications, and has the task to *transform* these energies. The rider's body is to absorb the energies coming from the rear, do something with them (affect change), and then pass them on through his shoulders, arms, hands, and joints toward the horse's mouth.

The body can be used in two different ways in these transforming activities: As *weight*, the body can tilt (1) forward or (2) backward from its perpendicular position. It can also tilt slightly (3) right or (4) left from the same perpendicular position. It can also weigh one or the other seat bones by rotating slightly (5) one shoulder forward, and the other (6) backward from their parallel position. These six weight affecting changes can be combined with infinite complexity. As *power*, the body can (1) flex or (2) relax some or all of the back muscles, thereby indicating resistance or cooperation, respectively, to the horse's offered movement.

In short, the body, the all-important instrument of transformation and control of the horse's movement, can either shift weight by varied tilting, or regulate energy by bracing or relaxing. These activities of the rider's body are to serve basically three functions of transformation: (1) either drive or (2) follow and harmonize as an approval, or (3) restrain by bracing. A rider should constantly be doing one of the three with his body. Furthermore, he should always apply the appropriate one. Most riders, unfortunately, only yield to the horse by following his movements, with which they seek to harmonize at all cost. These riders are travelers, and impotent as meaningful transformers of the dynamic energies entrusted to them by the horse.

The *hands* serve a double purpose: (1) they provide guidance and steering, and (2) they control the horse's mouth, which is the terminating point for his energies. Thus the hands are primarily a controlling mechanism. They absorb the excess that the boots create and the body cannot handle. As such they should be the least important, lease used, and most sparingly engaged units of the aiding syndrome. Correctly

Contrast the first three pictures with the last three. In the first three, the horse's mouth is deformed by a painful contact of the bit by the rider against which he defends himself by opening the mouth, tilting the head, and surely by running away from the source of pain. In the last three pictures is a mouth that is wet with foam, closed, and with relaxed lips indicating that the rider's contract is correct.

used hands should: (1) never punish, (2) be always as light and as inactive as possible, and (3) should be controlled with the back muscles and elbow joints while the arms remain relaxed. The rider's hands must depend on supple use of all joints starting with the shoulder and on down to the fingers. The wrists and fingers should act as tension springs to eliminate shocking (jarring) the horse's jaw. The arm muscles should be relaxed and not in use. Basically, the hands should be a mere extension of the activities of the rider's back, and certainly always coordinated with it. Therefore the hands, just like the body, will drive, restrain, or yield freely, as needed.

There are two basic aiding systems according to coordination harmonies in the rider's body. They must be used appropriately, and with properly effortless interchangeability. Riders must always be able to shift from one system to the other, according to communication needs. These two systems are sometimes called *unilateral* and *bilateral* or *parallel* and *diagonal* aiding systems, respectively. I will use the latter pair of terms when discussing them.

Using a *parallel aiding system*, the rider must act identically, do exactly the same on both sides, thereby affecting the horse identically on both sides. He must place the right boot on the horse exactly opposite the left one. He must use his weight and his back muscles identically on both sides of his spinal column. He must engage his hands similarly, and carry them in identical positions on both sides of the horse's crest.

This aiding system should be in effect when we wish the horse to use himself symmetrically in identical ways on both sides of his spinal column (be straight). The occasions when the parallel aiding system is in use are fewer than those when diagonal aids are necessary, and are limited to the following:

1. When the horse is to halt—all the time.
2. When reining back—all the time.
3. When trotting—only on a straight path.
4. When walking—only on a straight path.

When using a *diagonal aiding system* the rider must do different things on each side of the horse. Boots, back, torso, hands—all act differently on the right side than on the left side. Usually action is initiated by the boot on one side of the horse. Running through the transforming body of the rider, it will terminate in the hand at the opposite side from the initiating boot.

We talk about *inside* and *outside* of a horse rather than right or left. To understand this terminology is important for the discussion of diagonal aids. The *inside* is usually, but not always, that side which is toward the center of the arena. The *outside* is usually the one toward the rail. All the time the horse should be bent, more or less, to his inside. Therefore, if the horse is in counter-canter, he must be bent away from the center of the arena, facing toward the rail. In such a case the *inside* of the horse is actually to the outside. Where there is no rail (in cross-country riding, jumping through continuous curving lines, etc.), the *inside* is always the one toward which the horse is bent. Thus the horse is always shorter or *hollow* to the inside, and longer or *full* to the outside.

Now let us return to the specific techniques involved in the diagonal aiding systems.

The *boots* can be basically in two different positions on the horse's sides. The so-called (1) girth position is slightly behind the girth, the rider's toes being directly under and flush with his knees. The so-called canter position is farther behind the girth position, about two to three inches. In diagonal aiding, when one boot is in girth position, the other MUST BE in canter position. It is important to maintain both of these positions with toes well elevated, and heels sunk, which guarantees riding with fixed calves.

The *hands* may be in three different positions:

1. The *indirect hand* serves the purpose of indicating lateral bending to the horse. In that position the rein is held so that if it would continue beyond the hand it would pierce the rider's breast on the opposite side. In other words, if the inside rein is held as an indirect rein, it would connect the inside corner of the horse's mouth to the outside breast of the rider (if the rein would continue beyond the rider's fist). The indirect rein is therefore near the horse's neck (but never passing over to the other side of his crest). It is slightly higher and always passive. It may never be pulled backward. In all lateral movements, when aids must always be diagonal, the rider's inside hand is used as an indirect hand. It is passive in order not to act as a rein of opposition to the inside hindleg of the horse, which is to carry more weight in diagonal (lateral) movements than the outside one. In short, the indirect rein is merely indicating the degree of lateral bending to the horse.

2. The *direct hand* is used for the performance of half halts and full halts. It is the hand position designed to effectively communicate all restrictive (backward) actions the rider transmits to the horse's mouth. It is the hand that invites smoothly and gently at the horse's mouth to slow down and wait for the hindquarters to catch up with it. It is the only hand position that invites backward while also yielding forward in rhythmic intervals. To this hand the horse responds by supply yielding his jaw, poll, and relaxing his neck. Those activities rebalance the horse's navigational faculties, allowing the tonnage of the front to slow down, and thus the rear to catch up and come closer (the horse

collects: shortens his body). The direct hand connects the horse's mouth to the rider's waistline on the same side. While in parallel aiding both reins are used as direct reins, in diagonal aiding the outside rein alone is used as such. It is important that the activities of the direct rein be always controlled by the rider's back muscles on the same side. The bracing of the muscles in the small of the back and around the shoulder blades should cause the invitations of the direct rein on the horse's mouth, rather than any strain in the arms of the rider. This principle also guarantees a much-needed smoothness to the rein and superb coordination with concurrent aids elsewhere.

The *leading rein* is most often used on young, green horses to offer them exaggerated guidance when needed. The direction of the leading rein is from the horse's mouth toward the rider's thigh on the same side. Thus it is a rein pointing slightly away from the horse's neck, and slightly downward, indicating strongly the track on which the horse is to move. As the horse advances, this indirect rein position will no longer be necessary, and be replaced by an indirect rein.

Now that so much has been said about the aiding system, let me add as a summary that aiding is successful only if the rider offers it through a sequence.

1. Rider prepares the horse: warning.
2. Horse responds to preparation by attentiveness.
3. Rider aids into movement.
4. Horse executes the movement correctly.
5. Rider confirms it by yielding.
6. Horse relaxes and perpetuates the movement.
7. The rider harmonizes with his relaxed horse in desired movement.

This sequence takes a very short time to perform, yet all steps of it must be performed by both rider and horse. Should one of them omit one of these responses, the entire sequence must be reinitiated by the rider who repeats the preparation.

It is incredibly important to yield to our horses. Nothing should ever freeze when aiding; nothing should ever be locked; nothing should ever become rigid. Riding is dynamic—it is perpetual movement. Therefore it tolerates no rigidity, which is the stopping of motion. Should any part of the rider become stiff or rigid, the horse will have to become rigid. If any part of either horse or rider is stiff, the whole system suffers discord, and correct gymnastic development comes to an end.

5
The Major Tasks in Dressaging a Horse

Dressage aims at the physical and mental improvement of horses by natural means. Dressage is a gradual process of development of the horse's natural capacities through logical gymnasticizing.

All horses can be dressaged, for all horses are infinitely improvable. Knowing the goals of dressage, and the methods to accomplish these goals should result in the discovery that all horses can only be improved by dressaging. The fact of the matter is that dressage was used for centuries to improve all riding horses, regardless of their tasks. Showing dressage in competition is a relatively recent development. Dressage shows are invaluable in upholding the correct dressage principles, and for demonstrating how well the dressage ideals may be approximated. Dressage is most helpful for the jumper, the cross-country horse, the pleasure and trail horses, and the working horses.

Let us not forget that while dressage improves all horses in many ways, it always, furthers longevity and promotes soundness. Because of correct gymnastic (athletic) development, a dressaged horse will offer, in any riding endeavor, more useful performance days than one not ridden according to dressage principles.

All horses have more or less natural abilities that can be unfolded and developed through dressaging. Only through the classical principles of horsemanship and through the methods of dressage can horses be improved to the best of their abilities within a certain given time.

To be sure, there are many equestrian "achievements" shown without adherence to dressage principles. But they are not real achievements in the sense of the horse's potentialities. To be sure, many undressaged horses jump high. But they could jump higher had they been properly

Roderick Johnson of Las Vegas and Kathy Alles of San Diego demonstrate that even tired or hesitating horses will continue to negotiate difficult cross-country obstacles as a result of trust and obedience to their rider.

dressaged. They could also continue to jump high longer than one season, had they been dressaged. They could also jump higher and for a longer period of time happily rather than in panic and terror.

Dressage aims to improve horses on their own terms. Dressage knows no other time limit than the horse's readiness to perform a task. Dressage will not reduce itself to force, or to artificial means, for these can achieve only superficial ends. Goals other than the loving service of the horse, particularly the fulfillment of his inborn promises, are incompatible with true horsemanship. The two major goals of mental development of the dressage horse are the development of absolute OBEDIENCE and utmost RELAXATION.

Relaxation is an attitude that develops in the horse only through consistent kindness and patience by the rider. A horse relaxes as a result of perceiving the rider as a trustworthy, just, and kind companion; as one whose judgment proves better in times of crises and emergencies than his own; as one who never doublecrosses him, or jeopardizes his well-being. There can be no relaxation of the horse without a totally relaxed rider. A true horseman will leave his tensions and anxieties outside the threshold of the stables.

Obedience develops as a result of clear and consistent communications from the rider. Obedience is earned by the rider through being trustworthy. The rider must never demand that which is impossible to perform because of lack in physical development of the horse. Obedience is earned by the rider through patience and repetitious perseverance in showing the correct way to the horse. Obedience is gained by rewarding generously the correct acts and attitudes shown by the horse. Obedience is made possible by increasing the horse's attention span and his ability to concentrate.

The two most common enemies of correct equestrian attitudes that will inevitably prevent development of obedience and relaxation are FEAR of the horse and INCONSISTENCY.

Remember that the horse is never a scourge who metes out punishment to the delight of a masochistic rider. He is not the contemporary equivalent of "inexorable fate" of which the Ancient Greeks felt to be victims. He is not a full-time persecutor so many riders proclaim him to be. The horse is not an opportunist with a concern to victimize his rider; he does not consider it his major task to shame his rider in public. A horse is not a psychopath to be feared. If you still fear horses, there may be one of two reasons for it.

Many people cannot shed a genuine fear and hatred for horses that is based on unfortunate childhood experiences. However, they usually continue to ride to save face in front of themselves and their parents. They devote their riding activities to the revenge of their childhood scares, inflicted unwittingly, and usually by a different horse than their current one.

Others use riding as their own physiotherapy and psychotherapy. The horse will become a substitute for feared and hated people. He will be whipped, tortured, abused, cussed at, kicked under the belly, just because the boss at work cannot be dealt with in the same manner, though it would be fun. Also the wife and children cannot be so lavishly abused in a nice neighborhood; well, off to the riding arena, and let the horse have it!

Unfortunately, horses invite much more such unjustly misplaced aggressive behavior, than for instance, canaries or dogs do. The horse, being powerful, retaliates with a good show of indignation, but seldom hurts his rider seriously. So the sadistic rider feels honored by a much larger opponent than, for instance, his canary would offer to be. The horse can also be controlled by cruel bits and other means employed by the rider, and he cannot run away from kicks, beatings, and torture like a dog would. The ideal scapegoat is the horse, for he honors the dishonorable torturer by being powerful, large, and beautiful, thus the most desirable kind of antagonist.

Inconsistent behavior denies success. Most riders are inconsistent with their horses for two possible reasons.

Riders often, but wrongly, presume that their horses can and will read their mind. They presume that a disobedience can be dismissed by thoughts of "oh, how naughty," without wielding the whip, and the horse will "intuit" the thought of dissatisfaction. They think that the horse will "read" their thoughts as they pet him after he refused to step over a pole laid on the ground. They pet him ostensibly to "calm him down." Of course the horse refused the pole totally calmly, and is calmly planning to do it again, for he is so amply rewarded when he is refusing it. The rider really pets him on such occasions to cover up his ineptitude in dealing with the horse's disobedience. He is "saving face" by being "gentle and considerate."

Let us, however, never forget that horses, though they are intelligent, are not blessed with extra sensory perception. When you reward them with petting after they refuse a jump, they understand that to be an approval.

Other riders behave inconsistently on their horses because they respond to the horse according to their needs, not according to the needs of their horse, or the task of dressaging. So when the task of dressage would demand that they jump off the horse after twenty minutes of riding in order to reward the horse for an outstanding achievement, the rider will continue to work him another hour, for he needs one more hour of exercise, or showing off in front of oglers. Or the rider will beat up a horse on approaching a jump, just to show some admiring by-standers how hard it is to leap over a three-foot fence with a competition jumper of six-foot ability. The horse, of course, does not understand the unreasonable and painful interference with his correct approach to the jump. He cannot understand that the rider is riding according to his own needs, which currently include a need for undeserved glory.

When a true horseman is riding, every one of his actions is being consistent with the horse's needs, and dictated by the tasks of dressage. A true horseman will always gain the admiration of knowledgeable observers, and will never sacrifice the well-being or the education of his horse to impress ignorant, sensation-seeking bystanders. We ride for the horse's sake, not for the sake of the spectators.

6
The Nature of Riding

Riding was a rather necessary skill in past centuries when many people had to travel on horseback. Today riding remains a necessary utilitarian skill only in restricted areas of the world. However, the importance of riding as an ideal form of recreation is ever increasing. In technological societies yearning to commune with nature is on the increase, and more and more people wish to be "doers" rather than "viewers" in their involvement with nature.

There are only three forms of competition riding offered for world championships and Olympic games. Success in all three, the three-day event, stadium jumping, and dressage, are based on some degree of dressage training of the horse.

Departing from the classification of riding according to the three major competition areas mentioned above, I would like to suggest three different categorizations. One initially may ride as a *craftsman*. Later one develops into a *teacher*. With talent and perseverance as well as artistic ability, finally one may ride as an *artist*.

The *craftsmanship* of riding may be acquired by anybody. Any physically fit person, regardless of age, can become a skilled rider. To be sure, riding is an extremely slow sport to learn, and the mere acquisition of riding skills is very time-consuming. On the other hand, riding is a sport that can be pursued to a very old age. Some riders compete internationally in their seventies, while others continue to ride for pleasure even in their nineties.

The craftsmanship of riding is based on acquisition of correct riding skills and techniques. When the rider has a balanced, independent seat that can relax and liberate the body for independent muscular action, one of the basic skills for a craftsman's riding is accomplished.

The next achievement is the acquisition of a correct repertoire of "communication aids" that will render the craftsman skillful in determining his horse's actions. He assumes sovereign powers over his horse. Then he can decide to use his good, effective seat, and his correct aids to achieve specific goals. At this stage the rider is born.

Based on craftsmanship the rider may become a teacher of horses if he is talented. Not all craftsmen will graduate to this qualitatively different status. The teacher will be using his techniques successfully in training horses and preparing them for very specific tasks successfully. The tasks may be as simple as the creation of a pleasure horse or a good trail horse, or as intricate as the building of an Olympic participant in the dressage event.

At this level the great quality of differentiation from teacher to teacher is that of "feeling." Any good instructor can tell a rider, and tell him fast, what aids to use in certain situations. But he cannot tell *how much* to use. The rider's "feeling" of "how much" will determine to a great extent how successful a teacher of horses he will become.

A very slim minority of riders will become artist. They will be outstanding craftsmen and great teachers of horses, with numerous additional attributes that they share with those creating in the fine arts. They will use great imagination in riding. They will have novel and outstanding responses to their horses. Their feeling of the horse will be artistically heightened by insight. They will add a great sense of beauty to their riding. They will add to the existing knowledge of classical riding form and theory many of their unique achievements and views. Their novel insight and creative techniques will raise their performances on to highly artistic exhibitions. These are the people who are not only teachers of horses, but should be also the teachers of riders.

Riders on the artistic level should coach those on the same level, and those one level below who are the teachers of horses. On the other hand, teachers of horses can successfully instruct only those on the level below them, pursuing the craftsmanship of riding. Great artists' talents would be abused by teaching the craftsmanship of riding. They can contribute most to the development of a rider who is already an accomplished craftsman.

7
Riding as an Art Form

In riding, as in all other art forms, craftsmanship is prerequisite to artistic achievement. Without proper fluency of skills that are parcel to artistic creation, no genius can display his talents. Everybody can paint more or less. In some schools there is not equal to the production of artists who create art.

On its highest level, riding is an art form, for it creates something novel, unique, and aesthetic by combining elements of nature into a more favorable (aesthetically) position. It is creation, indeed, by virtue of purpose and planning. It is based on the totally skillful control of the instrument of art, the horse, which in turn becomes the ultimate object and subject of the art. Riding is not unlike painting, where the masterly control of color is transfigured into the colorful portrayal of the object of beauty, which in turn becomes the subject of artistic, aesthetic appreciation.

As all other forms of art riding also involves the continuous working of imagination, originality of ideas, and profound theoretical understanding of the art form. Let me invite you to look at riding as an art form in its particular relationship to objective reality and its representation.

A painter deals with animate or inanimate inspirational models that are three-dimensional in their reality. He represents them on a two-dimensional surface. There, framed into immobility, the frustrated object of inspiration freezes on the canvas, though with more or less successful optical illusion as to its original three-dimentionality.

The sculptor immobilizes his subject just as much as the painter is forced to do. But his medium allows him to represent his subject in the round, and thus the statue's three-dimensionality is not illusionary as is that of the painting.

In the art of the cinema the surface of artistic rendering, being the screen, remains two-dimensional, as did the canvas of the painting. However, an optical illusion of three-dimensionality is added more successfully than painting has achieved, due to technological craftsmanship. Also, a new dimension, that of mobility, is added to the subject. Mobility is denied the painter and the sculptor who cannot deal with it in their chosen craftsmanship. Thus the surface is two-dimensional, like in painting, the third dimension is illusionary, like in painting, but there is movement depicted, as opposed to both painting and sculpting.

In the art forms of ballet, gymnastics, and figure skating representation is four-dimensional, movement being added to a realistic three-dimensional appearance. Little is left for optical illusion. Ballet offers the chance to see a Rubens canvas's population whirl around invested with life and athletics a chance for Praxiteles's Discobolus to throw away his discus. However, the movements remained choreographed, planned expressions of music-induced emotions.

Riding as an art form is yet more complex than those most complex four-dimensional representations of aesthetic reality, ballet, gymnastics, and figure skating. Beyond the intricacy of ballet and figure skating riding involves the total harmonization of movements between two vastly different creatures, two live organisms of entirely different physical structure, biological functions, mentality, and temperament. While the horse remains the subject and object of the art form, the rider must not only be the artist, the creator of the expression, but he must also join his horse in being the object and subject of his art.

The tremendous challenge is overwhelming, for the artistic unit, comprised by both horse and rider, is to be sculpted and resculpted from moment to moment and thus, while riding, the artistic creation is dynamically perpetuated with elastic fluency.

8
The Process of Riding

Dressage riding is a teaching process. Successful riders must be successful teachers. Riding excludes drilling, compulsion, force, unreasonableness, cheating, cajolement, trickery, conditioning, and cuing-in. Riding is effective only when it creates learning in the horse. Conditioned responses based on intimidation, repetition, or artificial secondary stimuli, represent no learning.

All teaching, including riding, is based on communication. Communication must be both ways. The horse always communicates by his actions. The rider must cultivate his "listening ability" to the horse's communications, and once the range of those are understood, must respond to them appropriately. The horse is a persistent teacher, and he is delighted when he notices that the rider learned from him and understood his communications.

The rider also communicates to his horse with bodily movements. Being more intelligent than the horse, he introduces meaningful, stereotyped movements called aids to make his communications more clearly understandable. The rider, through reasoning, can consolidate his aids by consistency. The rider must be aware that he is communicating with any and all of his actions, even if they were not designed to be aids. Therefore do not be surprised if the horse reacts to something you inadvertently "said" with your body.

A good rider always communicates with his horse. There is not even a second during riding when he is not aware of what the horse is "saying" and when he is not smoothly, patiently, and clearly "replying" to the horse. Dressage is inconceivable without such constant flow of bodily communication between horse and rider.

The rider must be an excellent "listener." If he fails to "listen," his horse may become dull, sour, resentful, apathetic, and phlegmatic, or may become outraged and deceitful. Indeed, the best cure for such natural tendencies in some horses is the intensification of rider-listening to horse-talking.

A good dressage rider is *preventive*. A rider who "listens" to his horse knows things before they happen. Horses "tell" you that they will buck much before they do. They "tell" you with their body that they will stop in front of a fence much before they slide there to do so. A good rider can prevent most of that which is undesirable.

Good riders also are perpetually *instructive*, and therefore corrective. They will "feel" the horse's body and know how every part of it is moving. They will be aware of the horse's bodily position at all times. Consequently, they will be keenly aware of the horse's balance and rhythm. They will always feel when the horse is loosing his balance ("falling"). A rider will always feel rhythm. It will throb in his whole system. A rider should develop an "inner clock" that is constantly ticking. The clock is ticking "one—two—three—four" when walking. It is ticking "one—two, one—two" when trotting or reining back. It is ticking "one—two—three" for the canter. The rider must, in imagination, become mentally a horse. He must feel as if he were in the horse's skin. All these mental changes develop in talented riders. Others will remain merely skilled craftsmen, and never know what I am writing about at this point.

As in all teaching, *the pupil must be motivated to learn*. Therefore riding should be primarily a pleasant experience for the horse. The horse being naturally a running animal, he is in great need of exercise. He loves to move about, roam, and run fast. Dressage riding must always encourage these natural tendencies. On them are based all the goals of a well-schooled dressage horse. Thus, the dressage rider's ambitions being in perfect harmony with the horse's natural inclinations, riding should develop into a most pleasurable activity for the horse. The horse's natural desire to move freely can best be channeled by the rider through relaxation of the horse, which results in his obedience. The horse's personality is kept fresh, and perpetually revitalized if the rider continuously urges his natural forward urge.

9
Aids

Aids include only those human communications to the horse that are purposefully done. While aids may include the human voice, and rewarding with tid-bits while on the ground, I consider these two aids inadvisable while in the saddle. A chatty rider appears, and often is, ineffective with other more appropriate bodily aids. One who offers tid-bits from the saddle may be surprised by his horse asking for some when halting to salute in a competition; a rather undesirable result of inappropriate communications.

Riders have basically three areas with which to contact their horse. These are the legs, the seat, and the hands. It is important, however, to understand that these three areas act not only as contact areas. They can serve also as pressure mechanisms.

Thus, the seat, for instance, is not only in contact to different degrees. Not only can it be lifted out of the saddle, or put into it heavily, it can furthermore be heavier on either side, or well balanced in the middle of the saddle. The seat, most importantly, can transfer the actions of the rider's back with which the horse is not in direct contact. Only those riders may ever become artists who ride mostly through the use of their seat.

Leg contact, when correctly maintained, gives the horse reassurance. The horse feels, through the ever-contacting legs, where the rider is, and what he is doing. Ironically, the more nervous, fidgety, jumpy, a horse is, the more he is in need of a steady, quiet contact of the rider's legs. Much nervous anticipation can be tranquilized if the horse is assured at all times that the rider's legs are harmoniously moving with him. By virtue of perpetually contacting boots the horse is also assured that aids will not be startling and harsh by coming from a distance. Does not distance make the greatest difference between a startling slap on the face and a smoothing hand layed against our cheek? Horses will accept quietly attached boots on their side much as they accept the firmly cinched saddle.

The rider's legs can drive only by being more or less in contact with the horse. They will certainly have to exert pressure differently during halt, walk, trot, and canter. In addition to pressure the relative position of the rider's legs on the horses sides will be invaluable for clarity of communication. The amount of pressure the stretched legs can exert downward into the knees and heels is also of great importance.

HANDS cannot only exert pressure backward, but release pressure forward. Most important, their effective action is determined by their relative position to one another at different heights in which they are carried.

The most important principle of aiding is that aids must always be used consistently. There are really no separate aids. Rather, there is a coordinated aiding system. The rider's entire body must be involved correctly in this aiding system. One must never do anything with just the legs, or just the hands, or just the seat. One must always aid simultaneously with all three in such a way that the aiding system remains coordinated. Only those riders can become artists who can coordinate their aids correctly. They will not only communicate with all the aids simultaneously, and in coordination, but will "feel" the desired extent of communication necessary for desired results. They will not underaid or overaid, but rather find the minimum aiding effort that will yield the maximum results.

To aid with one's seat is a misnomer that leads to unfortunate misunderstandings. One does not really aid with the seat. One aids with one's *upper body* or torso, particularly with the back muscles. The weight of the upper body can be shifted from side to side, not ignoring its effectiveness when correctly centered. It can, furthermore, be shifted backward and forward. All these weight shifts produce important results in the horse's behavior as all of them affect his ability to balance the "composite weight" of himself and his rider.

The back can be "braced" by straightening and tightening its muscles and rendering the small of the back rather unyielding. The back can also be rendered supple and relaxed, and a rhythmic follower of the horse's movements. Thus, the back can retard or drive the horse. In short, riders work with their torso, particularly the back, while the seat, as the area of contact, merely communicates these actions to the horse.

The hand of the rider is merely an extension of his back. The hand should never act independently from it. As a matter of fact, the hands should merely communicate to the horse's mouth that which the seat is communicating to the horse's back. That the rider's hands always act in coordination with the rest of his body is not to be understood as a rigid hand, "frozen" to the torso, a hand that bumps and bounces with the body, due to unyielding joints. No part of the rider's musculature and joints in his arms should ever become rigid, unyielding. In short, the hands and arms of the rider must act independently and in relaxtion, yet always in coordination with the rest of the body. When the hands are correctly holding the reins they are quiet by virtue of their relaxed coordination with the body's balancing movements, and will affect the horse's mouth softly. Such hands will transmit to the horse's mouth the feelings introduced by the rider's body, particularly the actions of his back. If he braces his back, such a hand will adequately and softly contract, "invite back" rather than pull, yank, or jerk the horse's mouth.

One should always hold as short a rein as possible, while making sure that the contact arranged remains extremely soft and void of painful pressure on the horse's mouth. Ideally, for a most sensitive, most effective contact, the rider should hold the very rings of the bit with his fingers softly looped through them. But having arms much too short for that contact is the rider's greatest "birth defect." Therefore, cumbersome pieces of leather had to be introduced to supplement the sensitive human arm. Yet, if the rider succeeds in investing these leather reins with feeling similar to the living human arms, he will succeed with his horse. The distance from the sensitive human body to the most sensitive part of the horse, the mouth, has thus emerged as the most critical area, as potential creator of problems. The intimacy of communication, relatively easy to achieve elsewhere by virtue of direct contact between horse and rider, has been compromised by a piece of leather between the rider's hands and the horse's mouth. Typically, the failure to use the reins correctly accounts for the majority of equestrian failures. Indeed, riders who cannot surmount these difficulties will never succeed.

Let me add as a word of advice a sequence of images that might help riders in correctly using their hand aids. As stated above, ideally, we should loop our fingers through the rings of the bit for sensitive, live, immediate contact between our body and the horse's mouth. That being denied, we must think of the reins as a third part of our arms. The reins should be considered as a "lower arm." In our imagination an extra joint, and a length of arm that equals the length of the reins, must be introduced and attached as an imaginary organism between our lower arm and wrist. As a consequence you must think of the reins as solid and incapable of slacking and hanging. Think about them as sensitive and muscled, thus capable of tensing (flexing) or, conversely, of yielding (relaxing). The result will be that the reins will never pull, hit, ram, or jerk at the mouth of the horse. The reins will rather invite back on it by creating a mild tension that can be sensitively modulated according to need, when necessary to be used as restrictive instruments. Rather than restricting, reins should more frequently be instruments of yielding (allowing). They must periodically, as often as possible, indicate "opening" (go ahead) without slacking and thus losing contact with the horse's mouth. To the yielding rein the horse correctly responds by gently "taking your hand." When your horse thus begins to "hold hands with you" he softly pulls on your hands, so tenderly that your arm muscles and joints can remain relaxed. He should never "lean" on your hand, and use it as a "fifth leg."

The rider's ids must always be clear and consistent. That will occur if the rider can think as if he is his own horse (empathize), when he can feel like his horse does. A rider who can do that will often be seen lavishly rewarding his horse, while his brow is clouded, and his teeth are clenched. At other times he will burn the horse's side with a fast lash of his whip, while displaying a brimming smile. In short, an equestrian never rides his horse according to his moods and needs, but rather according to the needs of his horse.

More difficult than the wise bridling of our own moods is to feel empathy with our horse. A good pair of equestrian hands must feel like the horse's mouth. When riding, indeed, our hands must be chewing, yielding, opening, and closing, like our horse's mouth. Our hands must simply act as if they were a soft mold of the horse's mouth. They must accompany the mouth's actions like fine kid gloves accompany the versatile, nimble manipulations of our fingers. One may often observe riders, however, who do not live up to this important equestrian maxim. They will pet and stroke their horses immediately after a disobedience. The horse will rear, spin, leap away into a mad dash, with his nose to the sky. The rider gushes with endearing words and smothers the horse in a staccato of tender pattings under the disguise of calming him down and reassuring him. Had the rider thought as the horse, he would understand the meaning of his actions as they communicated to his horse: much appreciated, enjoyed, and admired his rear, spin, dash, and rush, and would love to have it often repeated for the price of further rewards. The horse will gladly comply. The rider will deserve it.

An equestrian will never presume that any horse has extrasensory perception. The horse cannot "read your mind." He will not divine "what you really meant" unless you really communicate that to him clearly, in his terms, consistently, and with actions understandable to the horse.

The Mechanics of Aiding

Aiding is done in one of two basic ways. One may aid parallel or their greatest extent in order to provide maximum usefulness to as patterns depicting the letters H and X. Parallel aiding refers to instances when the rider's legs, seat, and hands are affecting the same areas on both sides of the horse at the same time. The boots are positioned parallel on both sides of the horse, and so are the rider's seat bones, hips, shoulders, and hands. The areas of contact, like mirror images of one another, are evenly distanced from the horse's back bone on each side and are positioned at identical distances from the horse's head. It is important to note, however, that the strength of aids may differ from one to the other side of the horse.

Diagonal aiding refers to instances when the rider's left leg and right hand are coordinated in harmonious action differently than the right leg and left hand are at the same time. In such a situation all contact areas, the legs, seat bones, and hands, are placed at different points on one side of the horse from that of the other. Needless to say, here too the strength of the aids also differ from side to side.

It is imperative to remember that all lateral bending movements are created and maintained by diagonal aids. Longitudinal movements and transitions, however, are created and maintained by parallel aids, excepting canter. Canter is a movement in which, even on a straight line, the horse's right side moves differently from the left side. Canter being a diagonal movement, meaning that movement runs through the horse on a pattern of X (from outside hind to inside foreleg), the rider must accommodate that position in order to effectively harmonize with it, therefore assuming also a diagonal aiding position.

Therefore it is obvious that most of the times a rider who is aiding correctly, is aiding in the diagonal fashion. Parallel aids are only called for at times when the horse halts, is being reined back, or proceeds at walk or trot on a straight line. During trot and walk when the horse is moving on an arc (when ridden through the corners of an arena) he must for that duration of time again receive diagonal aids.

Sensitivity of the Rider

The rider's sensitivity toward the horse's disposition, mood, mentality, and ability, are just as important as his sensitivity to the horse's movements. A sensitive rider always feels where every part of the horse is. He feels the horse's rhythm and timing. He feels how much each joint and muscle is exerted. One of the goals of all sports is to develop the sportsman's awareness of his own self. An equestrian must add to this heightened self-awareness an improved awareness of the horse and his every move. Otherwise he cannot possibly identify that which is wrong, and cannot detect where it went wrong. Without such awareness he cannot correct that which is wrong and improve that which is not yet excellent.

A good equestrian is so much aware of his horse's mentality and the actions of his body that he can anticipate mishaps. Those who become equestrians on an artistic level possess the ability to prevent much that may go wrong before it actually occurs.

Sensitivity, on a minimum level, will determine "what" a rider will do. Sensitivity, on a maximum level, will dictate with exactitude "how much" of what a rider will do. "What" should be done can often be determined by mediocre craftsmen. Certainly by any good coach. But the "feeling" as to "how much" should be done is the privilege of the sensitive artist. There is the qualitative leap from craftsmanship to artistry.

Feeling for a horse and feeling of a horse are inborn aptitudes, or rather resultant of a combination of several specific inborn aptitudes. Initially, these aptitudes may be dormant. However, when inborn talent exists it can be developed. Conversely, those who possess no inborn aptitude for sensitive riding will fail to become great equestrians regardless of their efforts. Sensitivity of a rider can be developed by any good coach. But much more important for the development of sensitivity are the horses one rides. Ultimately horses are the most important teachers, precisely because they can best provide for the development of sensitivity in the rider. Therefore it is wise to start riders on old, knowledgeable "school horses" who can teach them the feelings of correct movements, and reward correctly applied aids with correct responses. Therefore it is also important for riders to work as many horses as possible. Much feeling can be acquired by diversification of experience (routine).

Each horse is a different personality. Furthermore, each of them changes from day to day. Their physical well-being as well as their mental attitudes are constantly changing not only from one day to another, but even during one hour of work. Horses, being individualized living organisms, will perceive and respond to stimuli. The moment-to-moment workings of cause and effect during riding, as well as their general interaction with their environment will result in ever-changing mental and physical attitudes of horses. This is the greatest source of fascination in the art of riding. That is why, for a sensitive equestrian,

Collected canter, performed by Mrs. Kyra Downton on Kadet.

Ordinary canter, performed by Mrs. Kyra Downton on Kadet.

no experience repeats itself. To respond correctly to such a variety of experiences, the rider should be schooled initially on a great variety of horses.Given that opportunity, the repertoire of his responses will become enormous, and should he have the ability to "feel" it will certainly be invited to develop to its fullest extent.

A specifically useful technique for the sharpening of a rider's sensitivity involves periodic blind riding. It is advisable that the rider should periodically ride with his eyes closed. First, of course, the rider should get accustomed to blind riding on short distances, and at the walk. Later he will be able to ride with closed eyes at all paces, doing both lateral bending exercises and longitudinal transitions with diminishing frequency of peeking. Ultimately a rider should be able to ride blindly even zig-zag lines in half passes at the canter, or should startle himself with a pirouette at the canter without losing direction. Of course, lessons must never deteriorate to totally blind sessions. Riding with closed eyes can be beneficial from time to time, but must not monopolize all riding.

We are highly visual in our perception both by inclination and by contemporary cultural training. Yet the parts of the horse that are ridable, his hindquarters (locomotion) and his back (communication of movement), are invisible to us when riding. The areas we can visualize on the horse while riding are his forelegs, neck, and head, none of which are ridable. By looking at the illustration, one can perceive the

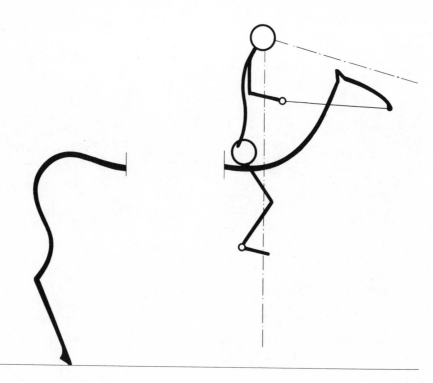

"stick" rider, riding the front of the horse visually, leaving his horse's hindquarters "behind" unattended. That which we are granted to watch on a horse is unimportant to the rider except for its entertainment value. That which we cannot watch, on the other hand, but must nonetheless feel, is what we must ride.

10
The Purpose of Dressaging

The purpose of dressaging is to develop the horse's inborn abilities to their greatest extent in order to provide maximum usefulness to man. Therefore, one dressages a horse to help him carry the rider in balance, to be flexible, rhythmic, and supple in his movements. Dressaging aims to make the horse respond effortlessly to tender, refined, consequently comfortable aids of the rider. Dressaging encourages trust in and therefore obedience to the rider. It also results in the horse unhesitatingly attempting the performance of any reasonable task the rider asks.

Categorization of the Horse's Natural Movements

Natural Movements	Longitudinal Bending	Lateral Bending
Halt	Collected (attentive) Relaxed (at ease)	
Rein back	Collected	
Walk	Collected Working Free Extended	Arcs, Curves, Serpentines, Circles, Spirals, Figure 8, Shoulder in, Shoulder out, Traver (rump in), Ranver (rump out), Half pass, Full pass, Half pirouette Full pirouette
Trot	Piaffe Passage Collected School Working Strong Extended	Same as for Walk
Canter	Collected Working Strong Extended	Arcs Curves, Circles, Spirals, Traver, Counter canter, Renver, Half pass, Full pass, Flying changes of lead, Serpentines, Figure 8, Half pirouette, Full pirouette

Gallop	Hand gallop
	Full Gallop
Jumping	High School (Haute Ecole)
	Obstacles

First of all, a horse must be rendered physically *balanced*. When he is balanced he can become flexible. After that is achieved, he will work with ease. While most dressaging is done from the saddle, much can and should be done from the ground.

Longeing horses and long-lining (driving from the ground) is an essential part of training. This horse is not longed for the sake of a rider but for himself. He will learn to balance not only on the flat but by jumping a simple pole on a circle without the weight of a rider or interfering hands. Work on the longe line is essential for the relaxation of a horse even after he has learned to balance and move with impulsion. Longeing may continue throughout a horse's athletic career, for it remains beneficial.

Horses are not perfectly balanced when free of burden and free to act. They are by birth crooked, bending more easily to one side than the other. They carry the majority of their weight on their front legs. They show awkward, discordant actions. They show a lack of awareness and understanding of their own bodily possibilities. They show no desire or knowledge of how to coordinate their movements into balanced, supple, relaxed actions of harmony and elegance. They are much

Mrs. Kyra Downton of Atherton, California, on the late Kadet at the walk, one of the basic primary paces TOP: *Relaxed ordinary walk.* BOTTOM: *An attentive extended walk.*

like a physically undisciplined, uncoordinated human being. Horses, being larger and balanced on four legs, show more deterimental effects due to uncoordination than do humans. Yet, it would all be well for the purposes of the horse. He would learn enough balance to produce

The Australian rider Andrew Rymill on his Hanoverian Avanti, working in England. His horse is at the halt in attention. While relaxed mentally, he is ready to move off in any pace requested by the rider.

A rider on a totally relaxed horse, which stands balanced but at rest. He will not move off with engagement without first having been longitudinally bent and attentive to the aids.

quick departures and fast movements in the wild, when that is called for in quest of survival. But when the horse is tamed and used for sport purposes by man, the horse needs to improve over that which would suffice him in the wild. He is capable, indeed, of great improvement, especially when such is called for by expert equestrians who give it sufficient time to develop naturally without force and stress.

When the foreign weight of a rider and his equipment is put on the naturally unbalanced, stiff, muscularly undeveloped horse, it will naturally profoundly disturb his ability to carry the now *composite weight* of himself, his rider, and saddle. The challenge of the dressage rider, then, is to establish *perfect balance*, and maintain it at all times under this unnatural composite weight condition. From now on, when I will mention the horse's balance his (his center of gravity), it must be understood by the reader to mean the composite weight of horse and rider. Once the horse has found correct balance under his rider, he will be able to move with relaxation and suppleness, both on straight lines and on curved ones. He can, however, only become supple as a result of improved physical strength. He will need to use all his muscles and joints with equal facility. Therefore, the "mobilization of the entire horse" is essential to this development.

Beautiful horses led to a halt. Much may be observed at the halt about conformation and temperament. Various degrees of tension or relaxation are clearly visible.

Arabian yearlings in Jerez, Spain.

Andalusian studs, trained for bull fighting, in Jerez, Spain.

Hanoverian gelding Avanti, excellent jumper and dressage horse, in England.

Condus, the Trakhener stud, in Gestut Putter, Iserlohn, West Germany.

Horses, having a long body, support their great weight on four legs. It is therefore important for them to place equal amounts of weight on all four of their legs for most efficient use at the halt. Humans also ought to distribute their weight evenly on two legs when standing, and they do it rather seldom, at times when standing at attention, for instance. However, it is well known that only in this position can a human being endure excessive tranquility and an effortless upright position for a long time as, for instance, it is demonstrated by various honor guards who can stand effortlessly, and without exhaustion. A horse, when halting "freely," is usually not using all his body, and certainly does not use it effectively. He is usually crooked and stiff and not capable of supporting his weight equally distributed on all four of his legs.

The suitability of a horse for athletic endeavors is seen in these pictures. Athletic horses have to be standing on a wide base, must have a well-built skeleton, must be well muscled, and must have correct proportions and angles in order to have natural balance and good basic paces.

The Hanoverian gelding Avanti, living in England, owned by My Rymill.

The Hanoverian gelding Avanti, living in England, owned by My Rymill.

The Hanoverian mare Julia.

The Hanoverian colt, born of Julia, at 8 months.

11
How To Dressage a Horse

When setting out to accomplish a task one must know the final goal. One must also know the basic methods for the accomplishment of that goal.

Dressage aims at creating (1) a horse that is *physically balanced* all the time while carrying the composite weight of himself and his

There is the wide desert of Las Vegas, Nevada. On it the relatively tiny points, the obstacles. There are no wings next to them. Yet the brothers Roderick and Ronald Johnson put the thread through the eye of the needle as they ride their horses over the jumps at a good gallop. This obedience, based on mutual trust, develops through the classical logic of training.

rider; (2) a horse that due to inborn ability to balance will *improve his movements* by shifting the majority of the composite weight to the hindquarters, from which all movement originates; (3) a horse that is always *relaxed* due to correctly bending his body; (4) a horse that is always *flexible* (elastic) due to the proper development and efficient use of all his joints and muscles.

Ideally, all horses should be dressaged, including those shown in stadium jumping or those moving across open country. Regardless of the horse's specialization for showing, he ideally should always be moving in balance, be supple, able to bend correctly, and therefore effortlessly. When a dressage horse is correctly developed, all his energies can be employed for performance, while none will be spent to cope with stress and strain.

Kathy Kostal of Las Vegas performs a miracle: a green horse that has never moved with relaxation and in balance under a rider, learns in a few minutes how to carry the rider with ease on steady rein contact. Since it is the first time for the horse, perfection cannot be expected. Yet, as a beginning, it is an excellent first step from which all training will progress.

The unbalanced, stiff, frightened, uncomfortable horse progressing with uneven paces.

Quieter, slower horse showing trust in the rider, who invites him to become comfortable and relaxed.

An appreciative horse first experiences how easy it is to carry the rider when relaxed.

Harmony develops between horse and rider. The horse willingly submits to the rider's aids, accepts the bit, relaxes all his muscles, steps deeper under his shorter, more compact body, and elevates his back, which has begun to swing. The goal has been reached: a relaxed horse moves harmoniously with even rhythm under the rider, paying full attention to her trustworthy aids.

Mentally, a dressage horse should show total trust toward his rider. He should yield to his rider's command, which he will eagerly await, will understand, and execute. He will be a relaxed, happy, confident horse who will be most reliable and trustworthy. He will show an increased ability to concentrate on his work. He will be calm due to trust in his rider, who will never demand of him more than what he can perform without stress. A dressage rider must pay particular attention to earning the horse's *obedience* through trust and relaxation.

To become trustworthy the rider should respect his horse's attention span. Never work a horse beyond the time of his mental fatiguing. The horse's attention span increases slowly, just like that of children, and if the rider demands continuous learning past the time when the horse's ability to concentrate diminishes, there will be resistance and tension.

Furthermore, the dressage rider may cultivate obedience, which results from the horse's relaxation. When a horse does what the rider requests in a relaxed manner, the experience will be synonymous with

Kathy Alles of San Diego, an outstanding rider, agreed to demonstrate what an interfering, stiff, unbalanced seat, combined with a rude, interfering hand, can do to antagonize a horse, destroy his balance, upset his leg order, and pain him.

The same rider on the same horse quiets and balances her seat and offers a light, quiet, sympathetic pair of hands. The result is a graceful horse moving with even relaxed strides in balance.

obedience. Relaxation can be induced in the horse only (1) by a relaxed rider; (2) by never demanding beyond the horse's current stage of development; (3) by rewarding each well-done move of the horse; (4) by aiding smoothly and only after proper preparation; (5) by using minimum, yet sufficient aids.

The fundamental principles of dressage riding are based on the horse's natural inclinations and on the dynamics of his physique. Dressage is based entirely on natural methods, as it promotes the full development of only the horse's natural abilities. Dressage employs no forceful means. It is a method based on patient encouragement of the horse's development in accordance with his own timing, in accordance with his own mental understanding and physical improvement.

Correct dressage must begin at the time of the horse's birth. The young foal must get used to humans and their handling him, petting him. He must receive the best of physical care, so that his development will not be stunted. Correspondingly he must often be in human company and his love and attachment to humans must be fostered.

At the age of one year the youngster's formal training may begin. By then he is weaned, he is gaining intelligence, he can coordinate his movements well, and he is curious and ready to learn. He will now be asked to lift his feet for inspection on verbal command or slight touch.

He will tolerate a halter. The yearling will then be worked from the ground. He will be led around and will be shown things. He will be talked to and touched all over his body. He will be groomed daily. He can be taken for rides in a horse trailer when his handler goes shopping and does chores.

After the above goals have been accomplished the yearling will be broken to the surcingle and cavesson. He will be longed and driven from behind on two long reins, or lunging tapes. The handler will stay ever so near his body, touching it constantly. Kicking will be avoided by the handler's proximity, while both horse and rider will avoid surprises and abrupt movements as a result of this proximity. The aids will be intimate, for the distance of the rider's voice, the gentle touch of his crop, and his affects on the reins will all be refined due to proximity.

When the horse obeys commands on the two reins, receives directions willingly from his handler, will halt, walk off, or even jog, he will be ready for further lunging. It is essential that the young horse be lunged in proper equipment. He will have to learn to move in all his natural paces and also halt on the lunge tape. He will have to respond to verbal commands.

When the horse reaches his second year of age he may be trained to pull a buggy. It is most pleasurable for an equestrian to drive a buggy. He can also achieve fine use of his hands, and the horse will now necessarily be asked to accept the bit and to handle foreign weight. While a two-year-old horse's joints and muscles are too weak to carry a rider and receive downward pressure, no strain or injury can be inflicted by having him pull a light buggy. Yet, very importantly, by pulling a buggy the horse is asked to learn many tasks that are rather advanced. He is to learn how to balance with a foreign, attached weight. He learns to accept the bit and the buggy whip as legitimate aids. He will learn to move fluently in all his natural gaits, and make transitions from one gait to another smoothly and without losing his balance. He will be learning turns. He will move straight, guided by the buggy's shafts. Importantly enough, during this training period he is getting excessive exercise that is so vastly important at this age. Exercise is now ordered and has logic in it. It is a period of work and concentration. Physically his joints and muscles begin to develop the way it is necessary to have them for the time when the rider will be mounted in the saddle. Now the horse is advancing mentally too. He is developing his power of concentration. He is asked to yield to the trustworthy demands of his driver.

When three years old the horse can be saddle broken. He will then be physically well developed. Mentally he will be calm, will love and trust humans, and will be able to concentrate and obey.

In all these stages of training the greatest virtues of an equestrian must be consistently displayed. He will have to be patient and consistent. He will have to spend much time repeating, sometimes punishing, always rewarding when possible. So it develops that before the rider sits in the saddle he has a somewhat dressaged horse, ready to continue as a fine pupil.

Once in the saddle, the rider can set out to accomplish the goals of rendering the horse balanced and supple under weight. Therefore he must address himself initially to two major tasks: (1) The horse must be taught the vocabulary of "aid language." (2) The horse's entire body must be "mobilized." The two tasks must go on, of course, concurrently. Without aiding, obviously there is no mobilization.

Mobilization of the entire horse means that the rider must demand that the horse uses all his joints and the appropriate muscles all the time and to the best of his current ability. Mobilization means that the rider must take advantage of the horse's inborn ability and desire to move bodly forward. During this period of training the horse's forward urge is not only encouraged, but when possible, improved. The rider must be primarily concerned with developing the horse's impulsion. This forward energy must be developed so keenly that the rider should be able in the future to "live off" the high power now fostered and accumulated. The horse must be made to go forward with infinite zest but of course not in uncontrolled running. He should appear willing to go out of this world without slacking or showing exhaustion yet in even, rhythmic and pure paces. You must ride as fast as you can without losing the *balance and clarity* of the horse's movements. This is demonstrated by clear and even leg order in the pace that is pursued. The moment your horse loses balance he will attempt to swing into a *potentially faster* pace, or will have unevenly lengthened strides in the pace now pursued. When you feel that that is about to happen, prevent it by stopping your forward urging, and brace your seat, thereby gently affecting the reins until the horse is slowing down to a balanced movement. You must slow down the horse until he is not only moving with clear and even footfalls, but is relaxing in all his muscles and reaches deeply under the saddle with his hindlegs. Once that is accomplished the driving may once more be resumed.

If the horse is allowed to pursue that movement only in which he already feels efficient, the road to improvement is barred and merely a status quo is maintained. Improvement is always based on requesting output beyond the already accomplished. At this initial stage one must always urge the horse to go beyond the largeness of the movements he volunteers. That is the only way the horse will be mobilized. Otherwise only those muscles and joints of the horse will be in use which he volunteers. That is insufficient. An athlete cannot be allowed to slouch about. You must not go farther than any athletic field or gymnasium to see how eager the athletes are in mobilizing themselves. They are flushed, they are hot, they got sore muscles, but that is the price of improvement. As long as the rewards are immediate, lavish, and offered eagerly, the horse will gladly exert himself, too. Mobilization of the horse is best accomplished by riding cross-country. It is never advisable to ride cross-country alone. The horse is calmer in the company of others and the rider is safer when potential assistance rides along. An older, well dressaged horse is the best company for a young horse. The more riders go out together, the better. The faster, nervous horses must be in front, the calmer, sluggish, lazy, phlegmatic horses should follow. From that order all concerned will obviously benefit.

During the period of mobilization the uneven, surprising terrain that has different consistencies and includes many ups and downs in priceless. Obviously, the horse moving on an uneven terrain will naturally have to mobilize his physique more in order to negotiate his task.

Never forgetting that the horse develops physically as well as mentally, the value of a varied environment is a most necessary complement to this initial stage of training. Thus the horse, during his physical mobilization, will also be mentally awakened. He will learn to tolerate the stimulus bombardment of his senses. Also, he will learn to concentrate primarily on his rider's commands, regardless of the environment. The length of this period of training will be necessarily determined by opportunity and not only by the horse's need. However, the horse will usually need three months of this kind of exercising, though it may vary with individuals. Cross-country riding for remobilization should remain the integral part of the horse's training throughout his life. The most advanced dressage horses will benefit from cross-country rides once a week. As the horse is being alerted and mobilized, his impulsion is being created, it becomes necessary to begin to bend him, too. Horses can be bent in two dimensions: (1) longitudinally, and (2) laterally.

Longitudinal bending refers to the horse being bent in his entire length. Bending commences at the hindlegs, the only sources of locomotion. It runs through the croup, and is communicated by a swinging back, through the flexed neck, to the poll and face, terminating at the mouth. This bending can best be imagined as a bow. The horse's longitudinal bending usually takes place in motion, the exception being at the halt, and therefore must remain dynamic. The horse is bent into an imaginary bow that shows flexion, yet remains relaxed. Flexion implies flexible tension. The imaginary string of the bow is connected from

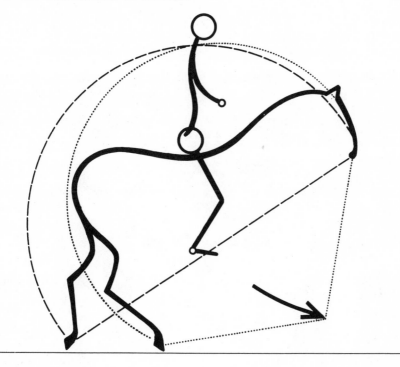

the hind hooves to the horse's mouth. The arch of the bow travels above
the horse's body and, when horse and rider are correctly matched as to
proportion, runs through the rider's shoulder area.

Depending on how tight the bow string is "pulled" the horse may be
stretched into a longer dynamic flexion (extension), or into a shorter
one (collection). The horse's activity within the framework of the bow,
however, must remain unaltered as far as the clarity, evenness, and frequency of hoof beats is concerned. All riders must create and cultivate
a built-in clock to count off the strides of the hindlegs. The timing of
the hindlegs must remain, indeed, as even as the ticking of a clock. The
rider must perpetually, mentally, tick off these beats. Riding is much
concerned with rhythm, timing, and evenness, and thus it is similar to
musical involvement. A rider without musical ability is handicapped.
Riders must cultivate the feeling of beat and timing as much as an
orchestra conductor, concert pianist, dance orchestra drummer, or ballet
dancer does.

When we bend a horse longitudinally, we may loosen that imaginary
bow string, flatten the flexion of the bow, and allow the horse to stride
longer and closer to the ground. Conversely, we might tighten the bow
string, according to the horse's ability to play along, and flex the bow

Here are three Thoroughbreds after about a year of training. At this stage they are diversified by a varied program of gymnastically sound exercises that include cross-country riding and Cavaletti work. The result is balanced horses, moving with good impulsion, carrying their riders well with swinging backs. They accept the bit, along with other aids. Their longitudinal flexion is well established. The three riders are from the San Diego area: Mrs. Kaye Norment, Mrs. Helen Polonetza, and Miss Kathy Alles.

more keenly, thereby shortening the strides of the horse. When correct collection occurs, it is obvious that the horse's strides are shortened only by virtue of gaining height. Slowing down the rhythm of the horse is NOT collection. As mentioned before, in this dynamic system of longitudinal flexions the hoof beats remain even like clockwork. Thus the shorter strides must never be slower strides. Sluggish, low strides that are shortened are a sure sign of a stiffened back. While an extended stride involves more the hip and stifle joints of the horse, the collected strides, by virtue of keener elevation in the strides, will tax the hocks and pasterns.

Horses moving in straight lines in walk or trot are bent only longitudinally (and not laterally). On straight stretches the longitudinal exercises consist of two major types: (1) maintaining the same pace (trot or walk) and *extending* or *collecting* the strides within that pace; or (2) making *transitions* from one pace to another (i.e., asking the horse to trot out of a walk.

Condus, the Trakhener stallion, at the working trot (TOP) and extended trot (BOTTOM), showing natural balance and fine impulsion. When the horse brings to the team this much, dressage development is easy. His excellent conformation, with generous neck, well placed and arching high, helps as a navigational facility to lower the haunches, engage more, lighten the forehands, and carry maximum weight in the hindquarters.

Mrs. Kyra Downton on a very young green horse (half Thoroughbred, half Hanoverian) establishes the longitudinal bending and submission to aids. The horse is moving in balance as a result, under the added weight of the rider.

The constant employment of longitudinal bending exercises, the constant changes from one pace to another, or the constant interchange of extended and collected modes of travel within a pace are of cardinal importance to the development of the horse's balance. It is also one of the most important instruments of suppling a horse. The muscles and joints are totally involved and mobilized when such exercises are done correctly.

To bend a horse correctly longitudinally one must remember that the bow string is adjusted only from behind. In other words, the bow may be tightened only by driving the hoofs nearer to the horse's mouth. The hands merely act as adjustive, light shock absorbers at the front. They may never pull the horse's face back in an attempt to "tighten

Lateral bending is called for even through a simple corner. Here Andrew Rymill trots Avanti through a corner. Clearly visible is how the horse is laterally bent to the right, his spinal column paralleling the arc of the path in an even, continuous bending. The rider's torso is correctly paralleling the horse's bodily position: outside shoulder for both horse and rider leads over the inside shoulder.

the bow." That act would inhibit the horse's forward impulsion.

Lateral bending refers to the horse's bending to one side or the other. His bending must be continuous and even along his spinal column. It should never be more exaggerated, keener, at one area than at all other areas along the length of the spinal column. For instance, the neck must not be more bent than the back behind the saddle, though obviously that is easy for a horse to do because of the neck's relative flexibility. Again, look at the drawing below. Imagine again a bow. The bow itself is a continuous arc that is part of a circle on which the horse is proceeding. The bow string slices the circle as it connects from the horse's mouth to the base of his tail.

Because the horse is a long animal, it is important that as he turns he should bend into curved lines, arching to the extent of the arc on which he moves. Otherwise he cannot possibly maintain his balance when moving through a curve. Needless to say that at the majority of times horses are asked to move on curved lines and only less frequently can we present them with straight stretches. A horse cannot move evenly through a curve without bending to its arc. To do so presumes suppleness that allows the horse to bend.

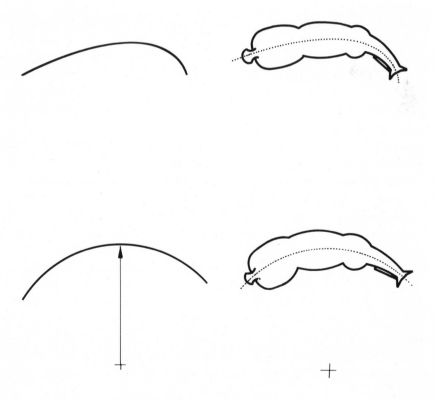

The longitudinal and lateral flexing of the horse must go on concurrently and must never cease. Throughout dressage riding both longitudinal and lateral suppling exercises must be pursued. Longitudinal and lateral exercises reinforce each other's development. There can never be any lateral bending without the horse being longitudinally "bowed." On the other hand, lateral bending will enhance the horse's ability to modulate his longitudinal flexion.

As examples we can say that shoulder-in exercises (lateral) will improve the horse's ability to collect (longitudinal). Half passes (lateral) will improve the horse's ability to extend (longitudinal). Bending in the horse (flexion) is correct only when it involves the entire horse, when it is total. Bending in the horse is dynamic (ever changing), because he does it in motion. This is the primary reason why the first task in dressaging , total mobilization of the horse's muscles and joints, should be achieved by virtue of impulsion.

It is easy to diagnose those horses that are totally mobilized and correctly flexed. The reason for that is that a correctly bent, and therefore supple, horse will always swing his back, and all his muscles will be visibly engaged in a rippling action. No impulsion can be obtained by just encouraging locomotion in the hindquarters.

Impulsion can be obtained only when the horse can and will communicate the locomotion of the hindquarters *through his swinging back* correctly to the front which absorbs and terminates that locomotion. Thus, when the energy created by locomotion is correctly communicated to the front, the horse's back heaves up and is lowered in even rhythm under the rider. Depending on the pace in which it is accomplished the rider's feeling in "riding this wave" is different. The feeling must always be distinctly there that the horse heaves up courageously under the rider's weight with his back; that the swells of the waves emanate from the back and "roll" forward under the rider.

The ability of the horse's back to swing is all-important. These back muscles are relatively weak. Horses in their natural environment had much less use of these muscles than others. Yet the rider's weight is placed upon them. The horse was not naturally equipped to carry that excess weight with ease. Often the weakness of the back muscles alone gives so much discomfort to a young horse while carrying his rider that he is incapable of relaxing. Therefore riders should work their young horses with short stirrups, taking good care not to overtax the horse's back by sitting his paces. Riders should post the trot and canter in "forward seat" in these early stages of the horse's training. That will put all the rider's weight into his knees and thighs, which pressure the horse near his withers where his back is the strongest. However, during transitions

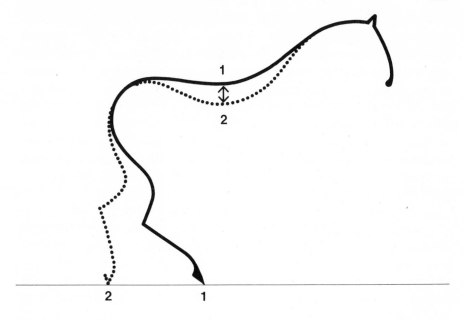

the riders should, even in these initial stages of training, sit down for a short while in order to increase the influence of their back muscles on the horse.

Increased ability of the horse to swing his back, to relax a strongly muscled back, insures the development of an ever-improving impulsion so necessary for a correctly moving horse. Therefore it is imperative to *gain the horse's back,* to encourage its correct use and thereby render it the proper and indispensable unit of communication from the hindquarters to the front.

The correct use of the back and the horse's ability to engage it will be served by any and all of the daily gymnastic exercises. However, there are exceptionally noteworthy exercises that especially encourage activity in the back.

The stretching of the horse is one of the most relaxing exercises that results in a mobile, relaxed, yet strong back. The back must be stretched right from the beginning of the horse's training under the saddle. It should continue throughout his sporting career.

When a horse is being stretched he is encouraged to extend his head and neck forward and downward. When this is performed, his back will elevate, "swell" under his rider, carrying him couageously, while his hindlegs will swing long and deep under the center of gravity. The movement will be low to the ground because it will be primarily supplied by the hip and stifle joints rather than those of the hocks and pasterns.

Stretching is encouraged by smoothly driving the horse forward with legs and back muscles while slowly stroking the reins backward and upward toward the direction of the rider's breast. It can be smoothly done by putting both reins in one hand and, as if stretching a light rubber band, gently and with a continuously "full" feeling, lengthen it by slipping it out between the fingers. If there is proper driving accompanying this action, the horse will react to that invitation by pulling the reins smoothly out of the hand, downward and out, in exactly the opposite direction to that of the stroking movements.

Another way of stretching the horse once more involves strong forward driving while retaining the usual short riding reins. Then the rider must begin to invite on these reins by bracing his back, thereby creating gentle but sustained pressure on the horse's mouth. After this pressure has been strengthened by the horse taking a firmer contact due to much driving and firm retaining, the rider must lower the reins with his arms

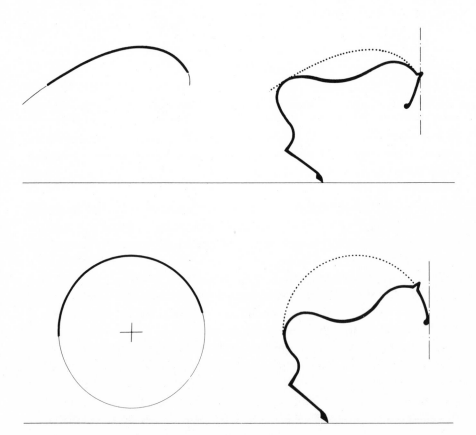

moving gradually and smoothly toward the horse's mouth, along the sides of his neck, without lengthening the reins themselves. To this the horse will also respond by stretching.

Stretching for a horse is just as important in order to relax, as it is for a human being. After sustained immobility or grudging stiffness in human musculature, we all stand up and stretch with joy. After that activity our muscles are relieved of pain, we relax, our circulation floods us with warmth, and we feel special strength in our revitalized body. This very same thing happens to a horse as a result of stretching.

Stretching must be done in all basic paces. First it is taught and encouraged at the walk. But then it must be done at the trot, canter, and halt, too. When a horse is well stretched and uses his back as fully as we can desire, he will seek the ground with his nose much like a hound following scent, and will stay there for a short while with his nose.

As the horse advances in dressage, and collected movements can be maintained by him, the importance and necessity of stretching diminishes. As the horse can produce no real collection without an enormously supple swinging back, it is presumed that he has by then full use of this part of his body. However, every time the horse is offered a spell of rest, he must be stretched out into resting posture all through his life. But by then it is not an exercise done frequently, but rather a natural beginning to the rest period.

Transitions from trot to canter and back to trot are another fine exercise for suppling the horse's back. Because the horse uses himself vastly differently in the movement of trot than in the movement of canter, when he is asked to transit from one to the other, an enormous ripple at the back absorbs the dynamic shock so necessary to change his posture, which produces the different leg orders. The frequency of changes from trot to canter and back to trot is the medicinal magic in this exercise. The trot is a bilateral, swinging movement, while the canter is a unilateral, bounding movement. Both demand excessive impulsion and express zestful forward urge. Thus in both the mobilization of the horse is great. While stretching encourages correct posture of the back muscles for carriage of weight, these suggested transitions do a superb job of strengthening the same muscles.

It is advisable to make these transitions in the following way: Always ride twice as many trot strides as you do canter bounds. Start, let us say, with twenty strides of trot, and follow it by ten bounds of canter. Reduce it to sixteen strides of trot and eight bounds of canter. Then gradually diminish, possibly over a period of time, rather than the same session, all the way to four strides of trot alternated with only two bounds of canter on an advanced horse. Presuming that they are done calmly by the horse and with light aids by the rider, these exercises produce miraculous effects in suppling up a strengthening musculature in the horse's back. This exercise is also one of the more sophisticated longitudinal bending exercises that therefore results in greatly improved balance of the horse and should be utilized as an exercise to create collection in the horse. In other words, it helps any horse that is moving "on the forehand" to improve his balance.

The recommended counting out of exact strides in this exercise is a serious matter. The rider must train himself to do everything according to planning and leave nothing to chance. The rider must check on his ability to do things on the spot where it is planned to have been done. It is well to keep in mind that good riders plan to do transitions at certain spots, or by counting strides. This allows them to polish their aiding system according to the horse's understanding. It is not enough in dressage to be able to canter a horse. It is necessary to be able to canter him at will on a spot that has been designated for that action. The rider must find out by doing everything at preplanned spots, how long and how much he needs to prepare a movement on his particular horse. This attitude will correctly encourage planning, purposeful riding, and proper preparation of every movement and every transition.

Establishing communication with the horse must be the other major initial task of the rider on a young horse in addition to the already discussed mobilization. It must be understood that communication should always be both ways. Not only the rider communicates to the horse by virtue of his aids, but the horse also communicates back to the rider. Both horse and rider must communicate perpetually when interacting. A rider who refuses to "listen" to the horse's communications, or when doing so fails to understand and properly interpret them, will never be a successful equestrian.

Techniques of Communications

Find out how the horse responds to your various aids. How will he respond to your weight, the movements of your back, the driving of your legs, the invitations and restraining of your hands? In other words, find out how much he can grasp your "language of aids," and in what respect is his "colloquialism" different from yours. How sensitive and attentive he is to your conversation will determine how much you will have to raise your voice to be understood. Usually young, untrained horses demand that you "shout" to them. On the other hand, if the purpose of dressage is correctly fulfilled, your advanced dressage horse will listen to and understand your most intimate "whispers." That is precisely why a dressage horse looks so effortless and executes movements as if by himself, without any suggestion and interference of his rider. And that is why a dressage rider on his advanced horse looks like someone inactive to the point of looking as if immersed in blissful meditation or prayer.

If your horse talks the wrong language, or is rather deaf to your conversation, you must adjust his mood. Review some of your vocabulary with him. Demand some understanding of your language of him by virtue of repetition until your language is understood. When aiding, do not continuously "pick on your horse." Silently harmonizing with a horse is a most effective aid. Continuous picking is a harrassment that will either aggravate the horse or render him dull to your conversation. Not unlike humans who respond to constant nagging by ignoring it, a horse will "go deaf," too, when the rider nags at him with aids. Should a horse, however, show negligence in acknowledging your legitimate aids, a quick whack with the whip should catch his fancy. As he responds to that the rider must reward him by silence.

Move the Horse "On the Reins" (Longitudial Flexion)

Establish impulsion by driving the hindquarters into bold action, which should not be maintained by perpetual prodding, but rather with only light action of the boots. Then brace your back, thereby affecting your hands that connect to his mouth, and with half halts terminate his impulsion in the front by gentle containment. Within this system a roundness of movement occurs that is the sign of balance. A well-driven, mobilized horse that will balance his movement will not run away when driven, "falling" into headlong rushing, pulling out the rider's arms. Gentle, repetitious half halts, while driving the hindlegs should be maintained, and that should produce the longitudinally flexed horse. With young horses the bow of flexion is rather loose, open, and free, the bow string, so to speak, just taut, the system lacking sternness and stress. Flexing a horse must always come from the mobilized hindquarters, and must never create tension.

Should the horse respond to an invitation to flexion by alarm, consequently rushing or "falling," the rider should gently and gradually invite him back toward a walk. When the horse is almost walking, drive him forward gently into the trot, gradually increasing his mobilization. Repeat this exercise until it is clearly understood that not speed, but rather balance is wanted by the driving aids. As a result of balance flexion will develop while in movement. As the joints and muscles in the hindquarters grow in the ability to create impulsion the horse will effortlessly bend to carry the weight correctly in balance, and then relaxed flexion will be achieved.

In short, a horse is never "put on the rein" (longitudinally bent) by pulling on his mouth. The elevated head position on a gently arched, relaxed neck is merely a *symptom* of the horse being "on the reins." The real cause of longitudinal flexion is the correct engagement of the horse's hindquarters. These must move in good impulsion, carry the majority of the composite weight, and therefore maintain balanced mobility. While a horse "on the rein" will always yield supply at his poll and jaw, he will do so as a natural result of balanced and relaxed carriage.

No more can a horse be ridden without gentle reins contacting his mouth, than without the effect of the rider's weight, back muscles, and legs. It is wrong to think that a young, green horse can be advanced by only using driving legs and back muscles. Riding consists not only of using aids. *Riding is using aids in coordination.* Coordination of aids makes the greatest difference between a talented, "feeling" artist and the craftsman. There are really no individual aids. There is only an *aiding system*, a coordinated, complex, sensitive system of dynamics. That system must perpetually involve the rider's legs, back muscles, weight, and hands. Not one of them can be omitted from the dynamic system without instantly annulling the entire effect of the rest of the system.

Establish Regularity of Movement

Balance your horse who is now "on the reins and ahead of the legs." In short, now he is a horse that moves only when the driving rider drives him to do so, and is moving precisely the way the rider instructs him to move. He is also moving as a total, round, dynamic system, and maintains his movements by virtue of coordination.

Make sure the horse's movements are always even, regular, and pure. He must maintain an even walk that is also eager and balanced. The same must be achieved in all paces. The best test for clarity and correctness of movements are the transitions. If a horse still rushes in trot after a canter, there is more to do before we can claim a balanced horse. Conversely, if a horse rushes in the trot before he "falls into canter," there is proof that balance is lacking. A horse that is balanced must move according to the rider's efforts. One that can be kicked into motion, ignited, so to speak, and then "navigates," allowing the rider to travel, is not a well dressaged horse.

The balancing of a horse must also come from behind. It is the result of adequate mobilization of the hindquarters in order to maintain sufficient impulsion that insures the horse's ability to carry the composite weight in the movement demanded of him. A horse that is constantly pushed from behind without the flow of his movement being contained in the front, will stretch out, move flatly over the ground, and will rush headlong forward. Such a horse is "falling" on the forehand. He is merely chased, and thus incapable of stepping under the composite weight. Therefore, if he wishes to avoid falling, he must be rushing forward under the increased weight and kynetic energy that has accumulated around his shoulder area. A horse, just like a human, will step under the weight he carries wherever it has shifted. We avoid falling by rushing under the newly developed center of gravity.

The natural, initial impulse of the horse is to run (pick up speed) when he is driven. He will, by natural inclination, take your hand and pull on it as he begins to use it as a "fifth leg" in support of his falling weight. Such being the case, the rider must brace his back on the reins, and sustain that invitation for a while without allowing the effort to deteriorate into a pulling contest. Because nothing must become stiff, rigid, and unyielding in the rider's effort, this bracing also must remain smooth, gooey, chewy, and soft, and must be juxtaposed with the ever-driving legs. There is no possibility to gain balance without constantly telling the horse that he can get it and maintain it by using his hindquarters more adequately. Balance improves as the horse is bending his hindlegs in all their joints until they can reach under the center of gravity, and carry more weight on them by crouching deeper. All balancing in dressage must aim at liberating the horse's front legs of weight, allowing them more freedom, and lighter, higher action. This will result in the elevation of the horse's entire front, including the heavy neck and head regions, while the center of gravity will be shifted toward the hindquarters. Their is no need to elaborate on how much stronger the bone structure and musculature is on the horse's hindquarters than at the front. He is, indeed, by evolution so designed that all his powers are in the rear, and only encumbrances, dead weight, are supported at the front.

A rushy horse, then, must be balanced by being driven forward, yet without accentuation of speed. He must be balanced by a braced back, and sustaining hands against the driving boots. When these half halts are successful in the front, the horse will begin to step higher and rounder, will float his body higher, and therefore longer above the ground. That shorter, but higher action will be accountable for a slower, more balanced pace.

As soon as some shortening of steps occurs, thereby slowing down motion without sluggishness, the bracing of the rider must cease (yield) to show approval. As long as the horse rushes on the forehand, and pulls on your arms, you must also resist and thus inflict some discomfort to communicate your displeasure. But as soon as the horse understands and yields to your demand by shifting his center of gravity toward his hindquarters, you must also respond by yielding to him. This game must go on in endless repetition until the horse understands how you can help him to a superior and ultimately effortless balanced motion. He understands ease and comfort as much as humans do, and soon will delight in your help that creates his easy balance.

Maintaining balance through transitions is an important matter. Unfortunately, some riders think that one can "kick a horse into a faster gear," let us say from walk to canter, or that one can "pull the horse down" to a slower gear, let us say from trot to walk. An equestrian, however, must remember that the canter is only *potentially* the fastest pace. Likewise, the walk is only potentially the slowest pace. We know that a well-dressaged horse will travel from point A to point C faster at the extended trot than in the collected canter, for instance. He will travel faster at the extended walk than at the passage, and so on.

So it is important to remember that we do not "shift gears down" to a walk, or "shift gears up to" a canter. We must always aid into all movement forward. We ride forward even into a halt. In a good halt the horse's forward urge is much in evidence not only in his impulsive arrival, in his manner of halting with his hindlegs well under the composite weight, but also in his readiness to zestfully depart from the halt into any desired pace without falling on the forehands. He will indeed depart from a halt by lifting the weight up, into suspension in the air, rather than pushing it forward, driving himself "into the ground." The forward urge of a horse must never be diminished, compromised, or discouraged. So, mentally, we must always "shift up" to the next pace, even if it is potentially a slower pace than that which we hitherto pursued. Let me propose some images that might help here: We canter, let us say on a straight line, and decide to halt at a certain point. In other words, we transit from the potentially fastest pace into the very slowest, immobility. We then imagine that the point at which we desire to halt is just a few feet ahead of a large stone wall. We then ride the horse "up against" that imaginary stone wall until his head is resting against that wall while the rest of his body is "pushed up" in a nice gathering behind that resting head.

Similarly, but less intensely, we must always halt the horse's head first in its progression, and gather behind it the rest of his body. Other than when coming to a halt, of course, we do not completely halt the horse's head in its advancement. For instance, when we make a transition from an extended trot to a walk we just reduce the speed of the horse's head first into walking speed and drive the rest of his body right up behind that slowed motion. I hope to emphasize that driving from behind must be maintained under all circumstances, including under all transitions from pace to pace. Indeed, I want to stress that the very last act in any transition is driving the hindquarters under in support of the weight. As suggested above, there are potentially two kinds of transitions: those that are conventionally considered as "shifting up to higher gears," and those conventionally thought of as "shifting down to lower gears." Indeed, there are two kinds of transitions, qualitatively speaking.

When transitions occur that slow down the horse's advancement, regardless of whether it is from a potentially slower or faster movement than the one preceding it, we must act as described above: drive the hindquarters forward to a slowed down front, and gather the horse into the new movement. When, however, from a slower movement we proceed to a faster one, even if that is a potentially slower movement, we must do something entirely different. We begin by gathering the horse. We begin by collecting the horse briefly into higher, keener steps with a braced seat and half-halting hands. Then we ignite the movement so that the horse will not lose his collection or weight-carrying force in the rear. Rather, he will lift up the weight from the ground and move off, roundly and suspending. The initial gathering through a half halt then is followed by the opening of the horse's front, in other words, a following, yielding seat coordinated with yielding hands that "open the door" to the higher speed.

Collection is not merely a shortening of the horse's strides. It is rather an elevation of the horse's strides during which great impulsion is maintained. This great impulsion and elevated stride creates the desired suspension, which is practically synonymous to collection. As great impulsion is utilized for the suspension of the horse, greater height of step is attained while gaining of ground has been diminished. Thus, collection must be very animated, with noteworthy periods of floating in the air. High, animated action is the purpose and the documentation of a good collection. The most elementary form of collection occurs when the horse bends longitudinally and thus steps "up to the bit." Collected paces develop by degree out of this original moment of flexion.

Flexion and the Horse's Natural Movements

Dressage insists on training horses according to their natural abilities and by gradual, patient work, allowing the horse to develop his joints and muscles according to his nature. The aids of dressage are based on a logical system of communications that has a more than two-thousand-year-old tradition that was crystallized by success. There is a table that briefly outlines a summary of the horse's natural movements. There is an inherent logic to the categorization on this table. Comments are necessary to explain the illustrations.

Categorization of the Horse's Natural Movements

Natural Movements	Longitudinal Bending	Lateral Bending
Halt	Collected (attentive) Relaxed (at ease)	
Rein back	Collected	
Walk	Collected Working Free Extended	Arcs, Curves, Serpentines, Circles, Spirals, Figure 8, Shoulder in, Shoulder out, Traver (rump in), Ranver (rump out), Half pass, Full pass, Half pirouette, Full pirouette
Trot	Piaffe Passage Collected School Working Strong Extended	Same as for Walk
Canter	Collected Working Strong Extended	Arcs, Curves, Circles, Spirals, Traver, Counter canter, Renver, Half pass, Full pass, Flying changes of lead, Serpentines, Figure 8, Half pirouette, Full pirouette
Gallop	Hand gallop Full gallop	
Jumping	High School (Haute Ecole) Obstacles	

The *halt* is considered also a movement in dressage. Certainly a horse
is moving before and after a halt and, while halting, must maintain a
muscular tension and mental readiness resulting from the movement

*Andrew Rymill of Australia, riding in England on his Hanoverian Avanti
at the working trot. The longitudinal bending, balance, relaxation, good
impulsion, and freedom of rhythmic pace are all well established in this
then-green horse. Horse and rider show concentration and harmony, yet
relaxation and confidence in each other.*

preceding his halt. That will enable him to depart into motion with zestful impulsion, showing great forward urge.

At the halt the horse must be balanced on his four feet, and flexed in order to depart by lifting his weight upward, rather than merely pushing it forward. According to the degree of his advancement, he must halt with as much weight sustained by his hindquarters as possible.

Longitudinal bending or flexion occurs in its pure form only on straight lines. When the movements are performed through any curve, even the corners of the riding arena, the horse is bent laterally also. As you can notice on the table, there is never any lateral flexion asked in halt, rein, back, gallop, and jumping. The straighter the horse remains in these movements, the better they are.

Lateral bending always presumes longitudinal bending accomplished. There can be no correctly bent horse on any arc of a circle without moving correctly balanced along his longitudinal position. Longitudinal bending is a result of correctly used hindquarters that sustain desired impulsion according to the rider's dictates. The impulsion is communicated through the swinging back to the horse's front, terminating in the mouth. This bending of the horse throughout his body, while in motion,

Mrs. Kyra Downton on her Thoroughbred Crescendo, performing the half pirouette at the walk. The horse laterally bends through the length of his spinal column in the direction of the turn. The horse is pirouetting around the inside hindleg.

affords him correct balance and ease in carrying his weight. Without it there is no chance in bending the horse adequately laterally, in other words, from side to side. Consequently, lateral bending is bending to the side, evenly along the horse's spinal column, when that becomes possible due to correct bending of the horse's spinal column into a supple, swinging bow.

Because correct lateral bending is based on the horse's ability to bend longitudinally, initially the horse should be ridden as much as possible on straight stretches, and made to flex into a system that terminates by his arching his body to the hand. When a young horse moves through corners and other curved lines, he will have to be slowed down, and differentiated bending aids must be given in order to create his lateral flexion in arcs.

A combination of longitudinal and lateral bending exercises is the best method for gymnasticizing a horse. Anybody who is familiar with the great amount and variety of difficult exercises performed during a Grand Prix de Dressage test in twelve minutes, will realize how much more work can be expected in one hour.

Riders should ride according to well-planned strategies. Horses develop only as a result of gymnasticizing. Riders should know which gymnastic exercises are appropriate for their horses at any given day, and work accordingly. Most of the time a great variety of gymnastic exercises is advisable. Only when a horse needs quieting or relaxation should a rider dispense with gymnastic goals until such time when the horse's tranquility is achieved. Most riders, however, expect results by traveling about on horseback aimlessly, offering their horse merely a constitutional, serving his circulatory and digestive needs. Much beyond this kind of negligence lies the beginning of building the great sports horse. Well-planned, constant, reasonable exercises of muscles and joints constitute the gymnastics the athletic horse needs.

The exercises and the way they are combined must depend entirely on the horse's level of development. Obviously a young, green horse will find it difficult even to shorten his strides while moving on a straight line, while an advanced horse will easily perform a piaffe and a passage, and make a calm, supple transition from one to the other.

A good rider, however, rides his horse so as to gain maximum achievement through a minimum of exertion. There are two basic ways to determine whether a goal has been correctly achieved or not.

(1) If a horse executes the required movement with balance, suppleness, regularity, elasticity, and impulsion, while remaining completely calm and light to the aids, the goal has been fulfilled.

(2) If a horse can make a transition from one movement into another

Mrs. Kyra Downton on Kadet and on Crescendo, performing the piaffe, a trotlike movement in place. The highest possible degree of collection is shown at the trot pace where everything moves "except the horse." Even rhythm, regular hoofbeats, all legs leaving the ground (forelegs higher than hindlegs), and the moment of suspension are clearly present. Haunches are well bent, the croup is lowered, and the horse is attentive yet relaxed.

without losing his balance, with purity of appropriate leg order in the paces, fluently, willingly, and without losing impulsion or expanding his flexion, the goal has been fulfilled.

When a horse does what has been asked of him according to the abovementioned conditions, it is a sign of such achievement that indicates readiness to go on, advance toward a new goal. Great care should be taken also that impulsion be genuine, and not confused with excess speed or rushing on the forehand. A swishing tail, lack of flexion in the neck, at the poll, chin, and jaw, all indicate anger, resistance, strain, and discomfort. While any such symptoms of stress persist no advancement is possible.

The mouth of the horse has to be "formed," "developed," "sensitized" by the rider. Horses in nature never use their mouths in any way the rider expects them to do when carrying the bit. Their mouths must be sensitized to become perceptive to human communications. A horse should never be forced to stop by pulling on his mouth. Pain inflicted there may merely urge him to run away from the pain, and he might go faster. A rider can never control a horse by his muscle power, regardless of how strongly he pulls, for the rider remains the weaker party who is also the puppet that travels on the horse's legs instead of his own.

Therefore a horse can be only controlled through mutually agreeable communications rather than by power and force. The mouth of the horse is a most important area of communications, and the most difficult to develop properly to serve as such. It can only be "invited" to become an area perceptive to communications of the rider's hand. This will occur if the rider uses his hands gently, and exclusively for communicating the efforts of his entire body. When the rider's hands do no more than reflect the movements and actions of the rest of the body, the horse is assured of soft, logical aids that are the natural result of coordinated dynamics of the rider's other aids. A rider should avoid at all costs to "reach in" and "get a hold of the reins" while his body does something else, such as being busy finding balance or otherwise contradicting the hand's restraining actions, such as by simultaneously driving with the rest of his body. The horse will soon respond to the correct use of hands by "offering his mouth" to terminate and cushion the enormously energetic movements that take place throughout the rest of his body. He will yield to flex his neck, poll, and jaw. The result will be a soft mouth that is "alive" and actively responding to the rider's invitations to yield, or the rider's allowances to stretch softly forward to "fill and opening." One of the signs of a forming or sensitized mouth, through which one can communicate and in which there is dynamic action, is the wetness of the mouth.

Horses differ as to the extent of wetness produced at the mouth. There is usually white foaming, frothing, lathering developing at a "well made" mouth. This is produced by relaxation. A fast-moving horse will often be lathered throughout his chest and forelegs with the thick droplets of his frothing, or will slowly ooze out long dripping saliva. Another will have a relatively "dry" mouth, showing white foaming only at the lips, which may indicate high sensitivity and a resultant quiet at the mouth, or at worst a phlegmatic horse. Much foaming and heavily dripping of lather, on the other hand, may indicate a highstrung horse, very keen at the mouth, as he is usually throughout the rest of his body.

Champing on the bit mechanically, turning the bit over in the mouth, putting the tongue over the bit, dropping the bit loose in a hanging position, are all serious evasions of the rider's hands. They are basic faults, hard to correct, and are sure signs that the horse's mouth was not "made correctly" to begin with. These horses do not move "ahead of the boots to the hand," and through their evasiveness cannot be dynamically engaged into an effective system, that is totally mobilized to accept all the rider's aids. They will be on partial aids, and be mobile only partially, therefore incorrectly.

A horse that is not "on the rein," engaging correctly to the rider's hands, is just as poorly prepared as one who will not swing his back. A yielding and active mouth is just as sure a sign of correct impulsion and total engagement of the horse as is a generously swinging, active back. As previously mentioned, if the locomotion created in the hindquarters is not being communicated to the front through a swinging back, there is no true impulsion. The horse is moving only partially. His engagement is limited to certain areas of his body rather than correctly involving all his body into a system. Similarly, if the horse's movement does not reach his mouth and is absorbed there into a flexible and dynamic termination, it is a sure sign of incorrect, partial engagement. A "dead mouth" that does not correspond to the activities of the rest of the body, indicates a "cued-in" horse, one that is not engaging because of natural, logical, and ever on-going communication from the rider; one that is a cued-in performer who recognizes meaningless signals and responds to them insufficiently. A well-dressaged horse understanding the "langauge" of aids as invested with "logical meanings" rather than understanding merely words as empty symbols that stand for mechanical reactions. A good dressage horse is a conversationalist and not an automaton. The difference often shows best at the mouth, though easily recognizable also elsewhere to an expert.

A horse with a well-made mouth is easy to recognize not only by the

Mental relaxation of the horse ensures relaxed contact with the bit. As a result the horse salivates and produces a certain amount of foaming, frothing, or wetness at the lips. Doncaster, the Thoroughbred of Mrs. Patricia Sullivan, is shown first at the beginning of his work with a yet "unused" mouth that is dry. After only a few minutes of work Doncaster's lips are already wet, a sign of relaxed acceptance of the bit. Finally, Mrs. Kyra Downton's Kadet relaxes on the snaffle with foaming lips. The well-formed mouth, the horse's acceptance of the bit as an aid, are prerequisites to all dressage activities.

aforementioned frothing of the mouth. His entire front end will be relaxed and yielding. His neck, poll, and jaw will show a great flexibility and willingness to yield to contraction as well as the ability and willingness to stretch forward into expansion. The horse does have thick and heavy musculature in his neck. It is not easy to mobilize, activate, and supple these muscles. Yet stiffness, or lack of engagement anywhere in the horse's body, will produce stiffness in other areas. Thus no good rider can ignore the importance of flexion at the horse's neck and claim that flexion is only important in the hindquarters, since that is the "engine" of the horse. Inability or refusal allow the rider's hands to be active will always have paralyzing effects in the all-important hindquarters. Thus the work will be partial, and slowly, stiffly grind to a halt. Any stiffness, anywhere in the horse, produces detrimental stress and strain on the entire system. Indeed, it takes an expert rider, coach, and judge to detect partial immobility. This is why so much remains uncorrected, and to the detriment of development and performance of the horse. A well-formed mouth is for the most part the result of good impulsion in the hindquarters, a swinging, relaxed back, and attention to the rider's aids. To the observer the mouth of the horse will most easily reveal the secrets of the rest of his development.

Specific use of a horse should be determined relatively late in his training. Depending on the breed of the horse, and also on his individual personality, he will be healthy and athletic for varying lengths of time. Correctly trained horses can often compete successfully until they reach eighteen to twenty-two years of age.

Horses should be handled from the time they are foaled. Regular, systematic training begins when they are yearlings. However, they should only be saddled up as three year olds, and from then on the majority of their training will be from the saddle. Not all of it, however. Any human contact in the box stall, or leading them around, and similar activities, are part of the total, consistent human communication they receive. Also, lunging should remain an important part of their activities throughout their athletic career.

Thus, the horse's serious dressaging usually begins under the saddle when he is three years old. By the time he is four years of age he will be reasonably well suppled both longitudinally and laterally. He will also be relaxed and attentive. He will be able to remain calm in all paces of locomotion, carry himself in good balance, and with round, elastic motion. He will have exuberant locomotion (impulsion) that will be communicated through a swinging back to the front, where it will terminate in a soft mouth. In short, he will be totally mobilized, and he will have impeccable impulsion. He will be not only obedient, but mentally relaxed, will be able to concentrate on aids to which he will respond unhesitatingly. He will be calm, but alert, will move ahead with a great appetite for life, and will trust and understand his rider.

At this stage of development, at about age four, the horse's muscles and joints will be fully developed for the purposes of jumping. He will continue, of course, his dressage training throughout his life, since that is a necessary foundation and complement to working over fences. No horse should be jumping higher than three feet before he is four years of age. It could damage his joints, tendons, and ligaments permanently. He can certainly move over open country before that age. He can be exercised over low poles, taken from a trot. He can be made to be familiar with natural ground irregularities, such as rivers, riverbeds, ditches, hills, logs, etc. But no real jumping movement should be required of him before he is physically developed enough to do it with ease and without damaging results.

Since outdoor riding, jumping, and dressaging continue concurrently, the horse's development will be highly diversified. It is advisable to test

Dressage results in obedience. Ronald Johnson, participating in combined events, demonstrates that his horse, Two Muggs, will obey. At the bank all breaks are pulled in by the horse, yet he jumps off obediently after the rider overcomes his surprise.

this diversification by competing in combined training events. These events test, in form of competition, the very diversification of a horse we now desire. He will show his level of dressage in the dressage court, on the flat on the first day of competition. Then he will move through open country and natural jumps, with courage, at a good speed. Finally he will show his stamina, obedience, and maneuverability on the third day by performing on an obstacle course in the stadium. When all three phases of this most diversified competition are well performed we know that our horse has been properly muscled, winded, dressaged, to the level of an athlete. He has understood the language of our aids, he has trust in us. He will be a sophisticated, strong athlete, and somewhat of an academician if he proves himself in these contests.

By the time the horse is about six years old, he reaches the prime of

Cavaletti work may be infinitely varied and will yield infinite value to both horse and rider. Stiff, hurried, resistant horses with uneven, tense paces need it as an aid for harmonizing movements, learning rhythm, paying attention, and improving observation. Here you see three tense, unbalanced horses moving with hollow, stiff backs, above the bit, uncomfortably without balance. Cavaletti work will invite them to move correctly while offering the rider a chance to create harmony through correct utilization of rhythm.

Ground poles at the walk.

Elevated poles at the trot.

Ground poles at the trot.

his life. By then, as a result of correct training, he will have performed well in combined training events. He will have proven that he has been well selected for our purposes, and that he has been well trained. He has been fully mobilized to the point of utmost diversification. This is the time to determine how we wish to specialize our horse. When he is six years old we must specialize him, for his training has so advanced him that his competition tasks are becoming rather difficult. These difficult demands disallow the rider to continue diversification. There is simply no more time and energy left for either rider or horse to pursue an all-round training program. Now the horse is well founded both physically and mentally. Diversification has served its purpose. With his athletic body and his improved mind, the horse can be specialized. The process is very analogous to human education. First the young are diversified in their knowledge of sciences and disciplines. That affords them a sound basis for choosing their specialized field. While for humans the choice is self-made, for horses the wisdom of the rider must determine specialization.

Thus, when the horse is six years old, he will be designated to pursue either combined training events, or stadium jumping, or pure dressage, and specialize in one of these to the highest degree of excellence that his natural talents and inclinations allow.

Cindy Deacon and Alice Coon of Las Vegas succeed in relaxing and therefore balancing their horses over Cavaletti poles. The horses look happy and attentive and carry their riders with elevated, relaxed backs. They move in good rhythm and with proper engagement for their level of development.

Cindy and Alice at the walk.

At the posting trot.

12
What Are Communications between Horse and Rider?

Communications must go on: (1) perpetually, (2) as a dialogue between horse and rider, (3) with a tendency toward minimization, and (4) with a result in specific, desired goal fulfillment.

Perpetual communications between horse and rider is synonymous to riding. Everything else is meaningless traveling. Communications should never deterioate to one-sided monologue carried on by either rider or horse, while the other is in a noncommunicative mental stupor. Specific ideas can be initiated and communicated, however, by either rider or horse. In either case a response, and answer, is expected. This on-going dialogue is the greatest thrill in dressage. It is the very activity that makes it a king of sports by involving not only the physique of the participants, but also their intelligence. Particularly perception, correct monitoring of communication, is the instrument of sensitive awareness that is indispensable in both horse and rider. As the horse advances in dressage, conversation can be intensified by the rider as his horse shows increased sensitivity and willingness of perception, and demonstrates a keener understanding by faultless and instant execution of any command. This is the goal of refinement toward which the rider must aim.

The *dialogue* between horse and rider will have to be a sequential endeavor. The sequence of the dialogue must be correctly carried out and preserved. Failure to do so will result in omission of certain communicative acts, and will cause a lack of understanding that can result in failure or delay in execution of the desired goal.

Correct sequence of communications, initiated by the rider, takes place in the following pattern:

Sequence of Communications Between Rider and Horse

Rider	Horse

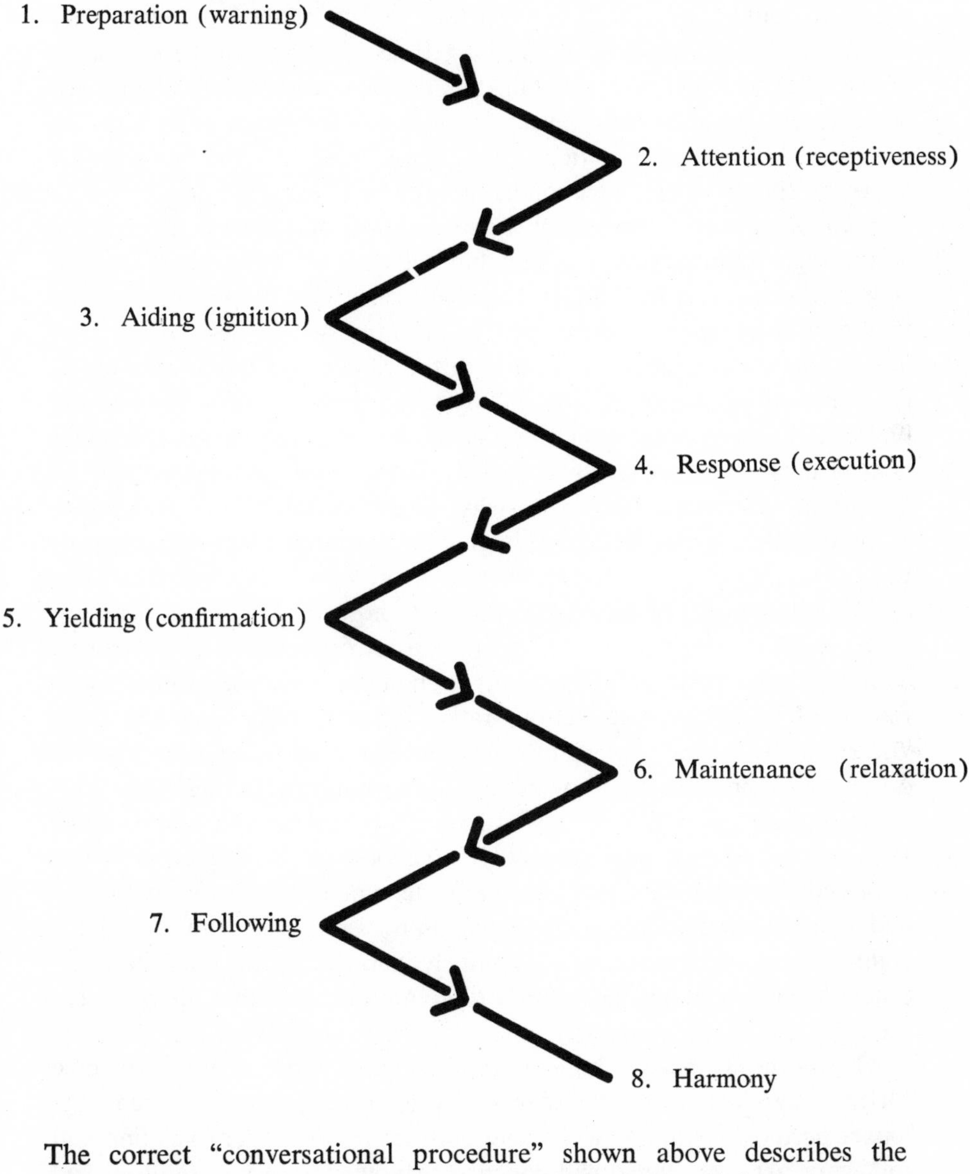

1. Preparation (warning)

2. Attention (receptiveness)

3. Aiding (ignition)

4. Response (execution)

5. Yielding (confirmation)

6. Maintenance   (relaxation)

7. Following

8. Harmony

The correct "conversational procedure" shown above describes the rider's initiated effort to achieve a certain goal in which the conversation is allowed to be dissolved in harmony. This takes a very short time. The rider must never go on to the next "statement" of his conversation without perceiving the horse's proper "answer" to the previous statement. Any failure by the horse to "answer" the rider, and answer with the proper attitude as suggested above, will have to result in repetition by the rider. Patient repetition in conversation of this sort is indispensable. The ultimate goal in dressage is to chisel an unfailingly polished conversation that is perpetual and consistently follows this correct sequence, yet over diminishing time. Without the perseverance of the rider to teach and maintain this dialogue there is no chance for achievement on an artistic level. His riding will remain on a more or less skilled level, with periods of helpless traveling and surprisingly annoying epochs of victimization by his ignorant, resisting horse.

Minimization of conversation between horse and rider must develop as dressage training yields its inevitable dividends. As a result of such training both the rider's and the horse's sensitivity to the other's conversation is going to be developed to the utmost. Needless to say, this is a development concurrent with both the rider's and the horse's physical potential to harmonize into one dynamic unit of action. Mental and physical unity of horse and rider is the most intriguing and brilliant goal of dressage. This is why a well-dressaged horse will act as if he is performing automatically. This is why the end result of correct dressage is the effortless dance of one unit, not the disharmonious struggling of two bodies pitted against one another.

At the beginning of dressage, while both horse and rider are learning each other's "foreign language," there is a lot of shouting and hollering without precise understanding. Many arguments develop that must await resolution by patient negotiations rather than by force. Later, a large vocabulary is at the disposal of horse and rider, allowing them conversation on a refined level and by intimate, charming whispering.

But conversation is not only minimized by refinement and volume. It is minimized also qualitatively. If you look at the sequence of this polite conversation that involves one statement followed by an eagerly and politely awaited reply as shown above, you will realize that the eight different statements are qualitatively, and not merely quantitatively, different ones. It is not the amount of communication that alters during the eight communication steps in the sequence, but also their meaning.

The more advanced a horse is in dressage, the less time it will take for the rider to perform the stages of preparation and aiding, and the longer periods of time he will spend performing the acts of yielding and following. Also the horse will concurrently develop faster attention and response, and will be able to longer maintain the desired movement in harmony. Obviously, it is the horse that determines to what degree and at what speed this qualitatively advanced development will take place.

Thus, the goal of dressage is then the minimization of conversation;

this quieting of the voices without compromising the resultant quality of performance; and this shift in emphasis from the production of the movement to the maintenance and sustenance of the movement.

Specific, desired fulfillment of goals is the paramount goal of all communications, whether horse or rider initiated it. The good rider is never guilty of delaying the horse's requests by misunderstanding them or by lack of attention. The good rider will perceive the horse's communication, and consistently administer the desirable response to that communication. Some conversation, initiated by the horse, indeed may elicit punishment as a response from the rider. However, at the majority of instances, rewards should be forthcoming. It is amazing to observe how in general riders remain stingy with rewards.

Should the rider initiate a dialogue without gaining the horse's correct response, he should patiently repeat his request. Punishment should be the last resort, reserved for occasions of willful disobedience or inattention. It should be instant, however, for delay of punishment may confuse the horse as to the meaning of that "sentence" in the dialogue. Rewards should, naturally, also be instant upon deserving. Even if it is a brief touching with the hand, or the relaxation of reins for a second's duration.

Once more referring to the table that shows the correct sequence of a dialogue, let us observe some important concepts. While the most important part of the horse's conversation is his response to the aid by executing it, the most crucial part of the human statement is the yielding in confirmation of what the horse has done satisfactorily. Riders who fail to yield their aids, legs, back, and hands, to confirm to the horse that he has done exactly what was asked of him, will never advance correctly in achieving the desired harmonious unity of dressage. I do not care how loudly you have to "shout" at a horse with your hands, or how strongly you must sustain some pressure to make him understand what you are saying, as long as you follow any inclination on the horse's part to understand you by instantly rewarding—even his efforts—with a yielding of the hand to him. A good rider yields so often, and so consistently, that he will never grow rigid in an aid, will never pull, press, push unrelentingly to "break the horse" into obedience. A horse will always resist when a rider stubbornly demands performance by force.

Yielding is the instant, ever-repeated response of the rider to any inclination of the horse to comply with his wishes. If a horse rushes and you brace against his movement with your back (and consequently with your hand, which is an extension of your back), he will slow down eventually. The moment he hints at slowing down and makes the first shortened strides, you must yield your back to him, resulting in the instant yielding of your coordinated hand. The results will be fabulous. The conversation depicted on the table will be continuing, and come to the desired conclusion: harmony.

You can never contest a horse by sheer strength. Obviously, he is more powerful than you. He is also much heavier. But do not forget that beyond his obviously superior power he has the physical ability to minimize the effectiveness of your pain-inflicting devices. He can drop his back low, elevate his head and neck, drop the bit off his sensitive gums, and take you really for a ride. We riders are a laugh for a horse that is fed up with us. If his superior power and ability to evade your forceful interferences would not be enough, let me remind you of his final superiority in any fight with you: you are on his legs. In a struggle based on sheer force, without finesse, you are his victim! He can travel with you on his back wherever he wants to, and at any speed he chooses. Furthermore, he can lie down on you, roll over you, rub you against a tree trunk while at a good gallop, and he can scrape you off his back with the aid of low-growing branches. He has it made.

No such war will ever occur, however, if you negotiate through the above described conversational sequence. You say something, he says something. You both learn to say the right thing in the right sequence. Never forget that you teach him the dialogue. You must do that through repetition, patient explanation, and consistent insistence that the dialogue is proceeding in the logical order. So, do your part of the dialogue meticulously, including yielding and following, and reward lavishly his correct responses.

13
How To Communicate Concisely and Consistently

When riding we communicate with our horses through our bodies. When working with them from the ground bodily gestures are to be supplemented also by voice.

Our bodily communications are transferred to the horse by various implements. This riding equipment is designed to increase the effectiveness of the rider's aids. Bodily communications, or aids, as stated before, must not be sporadic, but rather constant, consistent, and always coordinated. We must always affect the horse with all our aids simultaneously. However, some of the aids will be stronger, while others may be minimized. We cannot teach the correct understanding of our aids to a horse when we do not know them well ourselves. Not only must we know precisely what aids may result in what actions, but we must be sensitive in feelings as to how much of these aids will result in sufficient reactions. On each horse the *quantity* of aids will differ, according to his natural talents, inclinations, and temperament, as well as to the level of his current advancement. Furthermore, on the very same horse, the level of sensitivity to aids, and the desire and ability to comply with them, will differ from day to day, even minute to minute. This is one of the great challenges and fascinations any intelligent rider recognizes and enjoys.

Aids not only differ in quantity. While quantity of the aids must constantly be modulated to suit the horse's demands, we also must vary the quality of aids. One should not get a canter by kicking harder than at the trot. One must aid qualitatively differently for a canter than one has been aiding for the trot. In short, we must use and coordinate our body differently for the creation and maintenance of each pace. Furthermore, we must alter the actions of our body, the aids, when we go through any arc, rather than continue aiding as we had done while riding on a straight line. In short, there are different sets of aids for longitudinal bending and lateral bending. The horse bends all his joints and flexes all his muscles differently when pursuing longitudinal movements, such as halt, rein back, walk, trot, and canter. Similarly, the horse must be divergently aided to bend laterally into varied intense curvatures of different arcs and circles. All these are achieved by appropriate, clear, and consistent aiding. The purity and consistency of aids is so imperative for reliable communication that irregular aids, applied out of rhythm, are one of the most effective instruments of punishment.

Aids for a dressage horse have often been described in equestrian literature. I am eager to avoid repetitions of the existing literature in this volume. However, I wish to make a very short resumé of correct aiding, and add to these comments some possibly novel ideas.

As it has been mentioned, a rider may aid parallel or diagonally. During *parallel* aiding the rider acts identically on both sides of the horse. His weight is evenly distributed on both seat bones, his legs are in parallel positions, and his hands hold the reins in identical positions on both sides. This situation occurs only when the horse halts, is reined back, or when he walks or trots in a straight line.

At all other occasions aids are *diagonal*. That is, whatever the inside leg produces, the outside hand balances, and whatever the outside leg supports for bending and impulsion, the inside hand sustains. Generally, the inside leg to outside hand diagonal ansures impulsion and creates the prerequisites for bending laterally, while the outside leg—inside hand diagonal—creates the necessary lateral bending and maintains it correctly in the horse's entire length.

Aiding is an ever on-going process. However, the aids differ vastly, depending on what one wishes to communicate to the horse.

Halting is achieved by bracing the back against legs that gently assume a hugging support on the horse's sides. The legs must "halt" on the horse's sides by virtue of steady, hugging pressure that drives the horse's hindlegs deep under the weight he must support with ease while halting. Against this "reference point" of attached, solid legs the rider braces his back: he puts heavy pressure down his pelvic bones, which he "rams down" or "locks" to the very front of the saddle by firming the muscles in the small of his back, refusing to continue to follow the horse swinging back. This is supported by inhaling air and sustaining it in the lungs. The abdomen is stretched forward and the ribcage lifted up into a strong shield. The "bracing" travels upward, elevating the chest, the shoulders are brought back, adding a strong downward weight vector to the seatbones. Finally, the chin is elevated, which places the head and neck position slightly back, and proudly up, completing the erection of an unyielding spinal column.

It is important to understand that the bracing of the back is an act that involves the entire human body; that it starts at the bottom by establishing the point of reference with the boots, against which we brace our back. Neither driving, nor following, nor bracing with the back can be performed without having it done "against" the supporting attachment of legs on the horse's sides. Thus we brace our seat from bottom to top, terminating the movement at our head. The movement travels through the body gradually, yet fast. However it is not to be an abrupt, stiffening act! As bracing travels over our bust and shoulders it affects the well-coordinated hands that gradually contract the reins on the horse's mouth in a soft, backward "invitation." Such is the asking of the horse's head to halt the forward process and allow the rest of his still-driven body to gather behind it.

It is imperative to understand that a horse is driven into a halt, although it is done against a restraining brace of the rider. It is important to note that we halt "forward into" a brace. Bracing could simply never happen without it being ridden with strongly supporting legs that are stabilized in a hug on the horse's sides. Done otherwise, the halt will be incorrect. A rude hand, pulling painfully in order to make forward movement intolerable for the horse, will only make him creep into an unbalanced, awkward position. The halt is a movement. During it the horse must maintain a bodily readiness to depart in any pace on the slightest aids. Such proper rediness results from a correct "arival" into the halt. A proper halt may be considered an immobile act of transition from pace to pace, progression merely being suspended, but readily resumed.

At the *walk,* just like at the trot, the horse uses both of his sides evenly when moving on a straight line. Therefore it is logical to use parallel aids. At the walk the horses's ribcage will swing gently from side to side. During the walk the rider drives with his seat following the horse's back movements, which are long, flat waves traveling from back to front. He will drive with both legs, following with them the horse's rib cage, as it swings gently from side to side. The legs will breathe on the horse's sides, never leaving the warmth of the horse's coat. The pressure will be rhythmically "on and off" in its support of the hindlegs. The accumulated impulsion will be absorbed in the front by soft hands that follow the horse's nodding head movements. The hands, being merely extensions of the rider's back, must reflect the driving body's actions and coordinate them with following the horse's dipping head.

In the *halt,* similar to the walk, the boots are so attached to the horse's sides that to a spectator they will look as if they were painted there. No kicking, swinging, or other movement should ever be necessary. Here aiding with the boots must remain invisible and show leg tranquility that is in harmony with the general tranquility of the horse's actions.

At the *rein-back*, the rider must never pull with his hands! It is presumed that the reins are sufficiently short to act as a smooth, direct extension of the active seat. As the horse is halted, the rider must step heavily downward into the stirrups, and press with both legs, as if wanting a departure at the walk. However, the leg pressure will not be identical to the forward urging legs used for departure into a walk. For walking we gently roll our calves, so that the pressure applied has somewhat a direction from back to front, indicated by invisible "rubbing" pressure.

At the rein-back, however, the legs assert pressure while being pressed downward into the stirrups, and therefore offer a gentle rubbing from front toward back. By this pressuring leg position we brace our seat and tilt the entire torso very slightly forward until the shoulders appear directly above our crotch, which is well pressed down (as in all bracing). As we tilt our torso ever so slightly forward, our seat indicates a gentle "opening" to the horse, an invitation to stride backward to the area where weight has been lightened. As our torso is braced and brought forward, we necessarily lean toward a softly halted pair of hands. It is as if we "pulled" our torso forward by our two fists, which are motionless on the reins. However, that is merely an image; do not pull your weight forward by doing a "push-up" on the horse's mouth! On the contrary, the hands should retain a certain "forward look" as well as the reality of lightness that rewards each step the horse is making. In short, you press down and rub slightly backward with your legs. Against that attachment to the horse you brace your seat. That braced seat is tilted forward toward passively awaiting hands that have never pulled backward, but are merely held steadily enough to ensure that the horse cannot move forward. As the horse is being driven, but is disallowed to depart forward, he will quickly recognize that he can only back down, especially as that motion is cleverly invited by the rider, who releases weight pressure on the hindquarters, and opens up that region for movement by slight forward inclination. These aids must be meticulously coordinated, the human body acting as a lever or a scale whose tilts and pressures invite the horse to move in such a way as to counteract the rider's actions, and thus reestablish perfect harmony by a new balance system. As soon as the horse responds to the aids by backing, the hands must yield and the horse should continue to back on the leg and seat aids.

The *trot* is a dance that invites your legs to "dance along." I do not suggest dangling, hanging, anemic legs. I do not suggest banging, clunking, hypermobile legs. The boots are attached to the horse's sides, feeling the warmth of his coat, yet gently sway along with his rib cage and musculature. Apply supple, well-stretched-down legs, with all joints well relaxed, and accommodate movements by absorbing their rhythm.

The dancing, rhythmically supportive legs at the trot seem to move through a sequence. They first show relatively closed knees, then open knees to pressure at the calves, pressing eventually as low down as the human body can reach the horse's sides. Then through an upward ripple of movement the pressure area climbs back to the knees. So the legs dance as a rhythmic ripple that creates a traveling pressure along the horse's sides. The dynamics of this aid are cushioned at a supple ankle, which allows the rider's toes to gently rotate in and out—the heels moving in the opposite direction, out and in, and also sinking downward in a semicircular course. As harmony between horse and rider is the documentation (proof) of correct dressage procedures, the harmoniously supple, dancing, driving legs are an important accompaniment to the horse's lovely dance at the trot.

The *canter* is a diagonal movement in which one side of the horse acts and moves differently from that of the other. Thus, under all circumstances, even on a straight line, the rider who harmoniously parallels and accompanies his horse's movements and bodily attitude, will be diagonally distributed on the horse. I recommend that the canter be prepared with the rider's outside leg. The horse, moving into a canter, departs with his outside hindleg. Consequently, that is the leg to be notified to begin the motion, and that can only be done by the rider placing his outside leg first to aid.

In riding a general physical principle demands putting extra weight there where we wish the horse to stride in support of it. Therefore we must shift extra weight to our outside seatbone in order to create the canter. Since the dynamics of harmony also demand that we always parallel with our body the movement of the horse's body, we must rotate our outside shoulder back relative to the inside one, which will be slightly advanced, in order to parallel the horse's shoulder position in canter, where his inside shoulder leads the advancement over the outside one. Thus, while our inside leg guards the horse's inside shoulder from "falling in" from the rail and our inside hand is in "indirect" position to maintain correct lateral flexion, by rotating the outside shoulder and outside leg back for the engagement of the horse's outside hind leg, we automatically shift the necessary weight unto the outside seat bone momentarily, under which the horse is invited to stride. This positional preparatory act then will be followed by a quick impulsion aid with the inside leg, coordinated with the simultaneous push forward on the inside seatbone. The whole act may feel like a mild gyration traveling from outside calf toward inside knee while the abdomen lifts up.

During canter bounds the movement travels through the horse from his outside hindleg to the inside corner of the mouth. The swelling waves that communicate the locomotion impulsion forward also travel under the saddle from the outside rump area to the inside shoulder area. Thus, our harmonizing seat must pivot over the outside seatbone through a rolling inside seatbone toward a rhythmically closing inside knee.

There are two extremely detrimental faults I constantly see when observing young riders: (1) incorrect driving and following with the seat during canter; (2) incorrect aids when transiting from center into trot, walk, or halt.

It is essential for the rider's seatbones to stay always in the saddle during the canter, harmoniously following the ebbing and sinking of the horse's back. The rider should try to hold an imaginary dime under his seat, which should never slip off the top of the saddle. The rider should try to "polish" the top of the saddle with his seat by buffing it both forward and backward. The rider must "click-clock" back and forth in the saddle, never elevating his seat from it! Instead most young riders support themselves in the stirrup or at the knees, and with a rigid waist area swing above the horse. They rhythmically raise their seatbones off the saddle and shove it from way back to the front of the saddle, and thus create a most disturbing and strenuous thump on the horse's back. Meanwhile their shoulders travel enormously back and forth like a great teeter-totter. Needless to say, the whole action is stiff, forestalling any possibility for harmony, and discouraging the horse from using his back which he cannot relax under the painfully pumping rider's seat.

Instead, the rider must totally relax the small of his back. He must push his abdomen forward and lift up with it. His stomach area should be "emptied" over the belt to let it "all hang out," so to speak. He must hold the shoulders in a suspended position in the air. The shoulders should smoothly skid through the air without much rocking, and display tranquility of the bust and head. Under the torso, however, the enormous movements of the horse's back are accommodated by a most relaxed middle: abdomen, waist, and hip regions. The rider must sit in the saddle, not on top of it. He must remain in it like jello in a bowl. The abdomen must be allowed to loosely jolt as much as necessary, yet never swing the shoulders against a rigid back. By thus sitting supply in the saddle, never leaving its total surface and depth, the rider's seat will not only push forward on the swelling wave of the horse's back, but will also roll gently backward with one quick sinking to begin once more the riding of the swell forward.

When transiting from canter to trot, walk, or halt, most riders incorrectly stand up in the stirrups, or travel tensely into a knee support, and start to pull on the inside rein. Instead, the rider must create the transition by discontinuing the driving aid to the canter, which was a gentle pushing forward with the outside leg, alternated by a gentle knocking behind the girth with the inside leg. The aid is obviously diagonal, as it should be. The inside leg of the rider must swing parallel with the horse's inside foreleg. This is visually easy to check while teaching yourself to do it. When the horse's inside foreleg slants back pointing toward your seat, slant your inside leg back also to distribute a gentle knock on the horse's side. When the horse's inside foreleg is stretched forward, release all pressure with your inside leg, allowing it to travel, however, without leaving the horse's side. Simultaneously, shove forward with a gentle brush of the outside leg. At the time of transition stop doing all that with your legs. Instead, aid with your legs as you will need to aid in the next desired pace. For a halt, brace into a steady and strong parallel hug with your legs. For the walk perform rhythmic, slow, steady pressures, alternating with relaxation. For the trot begin to swing your legs in a gentle, parallel dance. That will indicate to the horse what you want next! Then, whichever leg aids you have given, brace yourself against the outside leg support heavily, pressing down your crotch from the outside seatbone. Brace the small of your back, but stronger on the outside, exaggerating the hold on the outside shoulder, which will create a backward invitation on the outside hand. On the very first stride in the new pace yield the bracing and follow with appropriate movements, never neglecting to parallel the now-even shoulder position of the horse by your shoulders and seatbone resuming parallel positions over the horse. Now, as you can detect, the horse is put through transition on a unilateral bracing limited to the rider's outside. The inside, especially the hand, must never interfere, for that is the hand of opposition to the inside hindleg, that very one that will need to swing under the weight freely and powerfully to support the transition. Any pulling on a rein reflects immediately on the hindleg on that same side by hindering it. It you pull with the inside rein the inside hindleg of the horse will be limited in its ability to stride forward. This must never happen when transiting from canter to trot, walk, or hault, for in each of the three the keen support of the inside hindleg is crucial.

14
How Should the Rider Use His Hands?

In dressage circles it is often considered unbecoming to talk about hands. The reason for this exaggeration of ethics is that we wish to emphasize that one should always ride with one's legs and seat rather than with the hands. It is true. Yet, it is necessary to talk about hands now.

There are no hands for a good rider, really. As I mentioned above, the rider's hands should merely be extensions of his back. If his arms are correctly placed, upper arms hanging perpendicularly and close to the ribcage, his elbows will anchor the actions of his hands to the torso. As the torso changes its position, and as it communicates the various attitudes of the rider's back and musculature in general, so the arms, being part and parcel of it, must and will follow suit.

The rider's hands must assume a variety of attitudes and must engage in a variety of actions in order to communicate in a synchronized fashion the attitudes of the rider's body. The rider's hands, as does his seat, may drive, follow, or restrain the horse's movements. When a hand restricts, limits, hinders, or restrains the horse's movement, it can do it basically in two ways. The restriction is carried out either through a *full halt,* or a *half halt.* The full halt refers to a total halting of the rider's hands as they reflect (communicate) the rider's seat engaged in an unyielding brace. This aid is, indeed, used to actually halt a horse. The hands in this case act identically on both sides of the horse, for the seat does the same. The hands, in a full halt, cease to accompany the movement of the horse's head, such as it is accompanied in both walk and canter. In the trot, where the horse's head is steady, both reins invite gently with a gradual, sustained, soft effect equal on both sides.

At a half halt one may coordinate only one hand with the braced seat.

But be it a bilateral two-handed effect, or a unilateral one-handed effect, a half halt never completely halts the horse's movement. It merely restricts, diminishes, and collects it. In a half halt the most important part is not the lack of following the advancement of the head, the gentle backward invitation, but rather the forward yielding of the hand that follows it. In a half halt we do invite back, but we release the restricting tension by allowing forward. In this act we always give back exactly what we have taken away. Therefore, a half halt merely runs a momentary restriction through the horse's mobilized system. It never hinders the fluency of the movement, merely gathers it, balances, adjusts, harmonizes it. Half halts can be brief, or sustained longer. They can be done very frequently. As soon as the backward invitation of the brace has produced yielding by the horse, the rider must relax the hand entirely.

Each transition should be preceded by a half halt, which is the proper preparation for changes in the use of the horse's musculature and usage of his joints. During a half halt the rider's back is used similarly to a lifting up of a tray of dishes. As the half halt terminates in yielding, the feeling is analogous to gently setting the tray back on the table. It is important to note that as the weight of the tray does not alter, whether being lifted or lowered, so should the pressure of the reins remain unaltered through the half halt. Only while lifting the tray (hindering the mouth), the rider sustains the weight. Yet while lowering the tray (yielding), it is the tray's gravity (the horse's mouth) that "fills up" the hand with weight.

A good hand is one that ceases to be a human hand and becomes, instead, a"horse's mouth." The wrist, the hand, and the fingers must begin to act as the mouth of a horse. They must become chewy, gooey, yielding. They must constantly stay together with the horse's mouth, never allowing the rein to slack or snap to unwarranted, taut position. The hands should be supple enough to maintain even contact. The wrist, hands, and fingers must act as tension absorbers, steadiers for an extremely even and soft contact, regardless of how exuberantly the rest of the rider's body moves along with the enormously mobile horse's body. The human hands must be such accurate and tender shock absorbers that they are capable of maintaining a steady, tender, but, for sensitivity's sake, taut contact. Their function is identical to the one performed by the sensitive tension spring that keeps the ribbon taut on a tape recorder.

A sensitive rider's hands on a well-trained horse simply fail to show movement. The lower arms, upper arms, joints at the shoulders, elbows and wrists are to eliminate any stiffness. By their supple functioning the hands must become totally independent from the dancing accompaniment of the human torso. It may sound like a contradiction that the hands must be independent from the gesticulations of the human torso, yet very much coordinated with it to the extent of becoming an appendage to the seat, while the seat must move independently from the hands when following the horse's mobile body yet not disturbing the horse's relatively immobile head. At the same time the hands must never act independently, for that is pulling; while coordinated with the seat, merely seat effects are logically transferred. A horse with a well-made mouth will respond to the simple tension in the arms and hands of the rider. Just flexing these muscles the rider will effect results in the horse. Conversely, by relaxing all shoulder and arm muscles, the rider will also effect the desired yielding when necessary. Therefore each rider must be very well coordinated and controlled in being able to flex and relax all or part of his shoulder, arm, and hand muscles.

The reins must be held as short as possible to connect directly to the seat. However, the rider must gather up the reins only after he has established his proper seat: perpendicular to the ground, shoulders well back, upper arms hanging relaxed, close to the rib cage in a perpendicular manner. Then reach forward from the elbows and gather the reins as short as possible to feel the horse's mouth gently.

It is very detrimental to correct communications to hold a very long, hanging rein. The rider must constantly pull on it to affect the horse's mouth. Such hands cannot possibly act simultaneously with the seat. They will be shockingly surprising, uncoordinated, rude, and always tardy hands. Many riders proudly display their "light hands" by dropping the reins. Well, their hands are not light, they are rather nonexistent. Yet, when they are used, they are rude. Another fault is to gather the reins from the shoulders. A straight line leading to the horse's mouth from the shoulders of the rider directly is incorrect. In such a case the elbows are stiffened, and the horse must carry these rigid, jolting, heavy joints at the price of disruption and pain. The upper arms must be hanging relaxed, perpendicularly to the ground, and the straight line of contact must be produced from the elbows, not the shoulders, to the horse's mouth. The rider's fingers must remain closed. Without that there is no sensitivity in the hands and they cannot act as a proper tension spring to the horse's gums. The rider must hold the reins only at one point: pressed between the thumbs and forefingers allowing the rest of the fingers and hands to conduct their miniature shock absorbing functions that are the essence of a constant and steady hand. The top of the hands should have muscle tension similar to that felt when squeezing water out of a sponge. The modulation of that muscle tension adds further sensitivity to the rider's hand aids.

15
What Purpose Is Served by Various Aids?

The *seat* of the rider is the instrument of balancing. To promote longitudinal balance the rider's seat must constantly harmonize with the horse's center of gravity. The seat must perpetually accommodate, follow the horse's center of gravity so that both bodies will unite in a composite weight vector that acts perpendicularly to the ground. This is why the rider's seat must shift, for instance, in acts of collection, or when the horse is jumping over a fence. The horse, instinctively will try to harmonize with the rider's weight vector. This tendency of the horse to step under the rider's weight in order to balance the composite weight of horse and rider must be utilized in dressage. This same tendency renders the horse most sensitive to the rider's seat, his primary instrument of balance.

In promoting lateral balance the rider's seat can shift weight unto the outside or inside seatbone, inviting the horse to stride deeper under his more taxed side.

Both in longitudinal and in lateral balancing the seat is connected by the hands to the horse's mouth, which by virtue of great sensitivity helps to clarify the seat's actions to the horse. As always, the activities of the seat are also, logically, supported by coordinated leg activities.

The rider's seat consists of two qualitatively different acting areas. The seat that touches the saddle on three points of contact uses weight effects to harmonize with the horse's center of gravity or by shifting weight to invite the horse to shift his center of gravity under the rider's.

The rest of the seat reflects the activity of the rider's back muscles, particularly those of the small of the back, above the waist. These muscles can tense into bracing, making the seat heavier. They can relax into supple following activity, approving the horse's current action, or powerfully shift the seat, consisting of the two seat bones and the crotch, into driving action.

The *legs* of the rider are instruments of driving and of bending. The rider's legs must always drive. They are often relatively inactive, and at such times are considered legs of maintenance. However, these maintaining legs are also active by remaining constantly in steady touch with the horse's sides, and in readiness to resume active driving. Legs are the most important creators of impulsion, although, naturally, synchronized with the activities of the seat and hands. The legs constantly drive, stronger to create new impulsion or activity, following gently when maintaining desired activity. They propel the horse both in longitudinal and in lateral action.

The legs help bend the horse when lateral action is required. However, they continue to fulfill their function to create and maintain impulsion. Lateral bending activities by the legs must be in addition to their paramount function, which is driving. Impulsion must be created and maintained constantly. Impulsion refers to the horse's hindquarters' activity that propels the horse forward. Impulsion refers not only to the activity of the joints in the horse's hindquarters. It also refers to equally eager, roundly coordinated activity of the joints in the horse's hindquarters. Thus it is not enough that the horse moves forward. He must be developed so that he can move forward correctly. That is to create motion that is coordinated, round, keen, bold, and eager, because all the joints in the hindquarters are contributing their necessary share to the desired motion.

The rider's legs always act parallel at the halt, rein-back, and at the walk and trot on a straight line. They are placed at the same point on both sides of the horse. However, at all other instances, the rider's legs are not placed parallel. They must, in other words, aid laterally. In lateral aiding it is the inside leg of the rider that always must maintain impulsion. The outside leg of the rider is engaged in controlling the hindquarters in the desired lateral flexion, while the inside leg maintains bending in the horse's body. Thus the inside leg is extremely active and rhythmic in lateral aiding. The outside leg, on the other hand, will be steadily leaning in sustained pressure against the horse's side. The inside, driving leg will always remain where it was in the parallel position, that is just behind the girth. The outside, bending, guarding, leaning, pressing leg, however, will be placed about one to two inches (depending on the intensity of bending) behind the position of the inside leg.

The *hands* of the rider are instruments of control and of steering. As the horse's long body is led by his head, obviously we must first indicate a change of direction with our hands. The activities of the hand being minor, but intimately connected to our body, our bodily position through the steady elbows, coordinated with the position of steering hands, will change. Our body having turned lightly, or having shifted weight to one side, will then have to be coordinated with our legs, which will assume their newly acquired position last. All this is to be done in a fraction of a second, and smoothly coordinated.

Our hands are instruments of control. They control the horse both in lateral and in longitudinal flexion. In their controlling functions, however, the hands do not initiate action, as they did when steering. Rather, when controlling the horse's speed, balance, or bending, the hands act last. The horse is driven first by the legs. The seat follows in order to harmonize with the newly created center of gravity. Lastly, the hands, being connected to the seat, will gently cushion the excesses created by the legs. Should the horse overreact to the legs by lengthening his strides when not desired, or by rushing (as a result of falling on the forehands because the legs shoved his center of gravity there), we must brace into retardation with our seat. Consequently, our hands will gently contract, limiting the forward activity of the horse's head, and that will create flexion, which will indicate that our horse found his balance in the desired impulsion.

In lateral bending the rider's inside hand will cushion the excesses created by the outside leg. Conversely, with the outside hand he will cushion the excesses created by the inside leg. Thus, as the function of the inside leg of the rider differs from that of the outside, obviously the controlling activities of the rider's hands will differ from side to side. As you recall, the rider's inside leg is the one creating and maintaining impulsion. Correspondingly, the rider's outside hand will control the longitudinal flexion. It will also indicate how much speed is asked for, and limit the horse to that speed, and to the desired length of strides. The outside leg, as you recall, had established the intensity of bending in lateral movements, and thus the corresponding inside hand will have to function maintaining and controlling the correct bending of the horse throughout the length of his body. Overbending a horse at his neck, while he remains relatively less bent behind his withers, is a great fault! It may force the horse to step with his outside hindleg off the desired arc. Thus the horse will not be moving through an arc by bending. He will rather "fall through" the circle in a lost balance, usually rushing. He will remain relatively straight throughout his body, with the exception of his neck area. He will "skid through" curved lines, basically pivoting around the point under the rider's seat: he will fall on his inside shoulder while swinging his rump out. He will go through turns like automobiles do. Observe the springs and tires of a car in a turn. Is its weight evenly distributed on all four tires? No! But the horse's weight should be evenly distributed on all four of his legs when going through a turn, for he can bend, while a car cannot. If the horse is not bending evenly and in the entirety of his body through curves, he cannot carry even weight on all four of his legs. Having no springs like a car, to balance off excess weight pressure, he will not be able to maintain a steady rhythm through a curve as a car can. He will speed up, lose his balance, his harmony. He will be uncomfortable and less controllable than he was on a straight line. Worst of all, some of his joints will be overtaxed and slowly injure him, shortening his useful service expectancy.

The rider's hands must be very supple and very sensitive, and superbly coordinated. They deal with the most sensitive area of the horse, his mouth. They have very important functions, and those must be coordinated not only with the driving leg and balancing seat, but with each other. Most of the time the double function of steering and controlling flexion is simultaneously called for. The development of good hands is the hardest for a rider to achieve. Unfortunately, most trainers, instructors, and coaches dodge the responsibility either because they don't know enough about the correct use of hands, or if they do have no patience to communicate it to the rider. Riders cannot have good hands before having acquired a balanced and independent seat. The very last stage in the acquisition of riding skills is the development of a perfect hand, and that stage often is just not reached. Riders who could not acquire good hands will always remain unacommplished, and will always harm their horses. They might, unfortunately, achieve victories in competition, when bid against equally unaccomplished competitors, or by virtue of luck. But steadily reliable excellent results cannot be achieved without fine hands. Consistent achievement that is by design rather than by chance, will never come without perfected hands.

Do not get the impression that hands are more important aids than legs or seat. They are equally important. However, legs being more brutal in order to be effective, and being connected to the less sensitive sides of the horse, cannot do nearly as much harm when wrongly used as hands can do. Failure to develop good hands will diminish the effectiveness of legs and seat because there will never be harmonious coordination among the three aiding instruments. This is why I spend so much time discussing hands.

There are three basic hand positions. The rider must be able to change from one to another within the fraction of a second. At times of diagonal aiding he must also be able to maintain two different hand positions simultaneously on the two different sides of the horse. Basically the hands can fulfill the same three functions that the seat fulfills. Remember, the hands are merely extensions of the seat when correctly used. They not only must act instantly when the seat does, but also in utmost coordination with it. They also must reflect the exact degree of the strength of the seat's aid. Thus, the hands, just like the seat, can retard, follow, or drive.

Retarding hands will communicate to the horse's mouth the bracing of the rider's back. By bracing the back the rider's hands must necessarily come back, sway from the horse's mouth if the position of shoulder and elbow joints do not change. In addition, one can retard with the hands further by tensing all muscles in the arms, but not to the level of rigidity or paralysis. More retardation can be effected by slightly bending the hand inward at the supple tension-spring, the wrist. As the pressure builds gradually on the horse's mouth, it halts movement that previously accompanied his head. Only in the trot is the horse's head so steady that relatively passive hands can accompany it.

Whether retardation at the hands is the mild contraction resultant from the braced back, or whether strength is increased by the tensing of arm and hand muscles, or intensified to the ultimate when the wrist is slightly bent, it always has to be released as soon as the horse has yielded! You can take a lot away from a horse as long as you always give it back to him as soon as he yields to your demand. Never pull after the horse slows down or flexes correctly, whichever you want to achieve. Hands, then, must not only be coordinated with the seat, but must be as gentle as possible, and eager to yield to the horse. It is the yielding of the hand that enriches its effectiveness, not the periods of tension that begin the activity. The periods of tension must be very gradual, sensitive, and alive with gooeyness and chewyness. Remember that your hand, when correct, thinks and feels like the mouth of a horse. The feeling most often should be as if you stretch a rubber band, or squeeze water out of a very thick sponge. In other words, the pulling is analogous to a soft stretching, yielding feeling, as the horse dynamically accommodates it. Sure enough, on a young horse the rubber band may feel as thick as a girth, or the sponge huge and heavy with water, but they still must have a tendency to give.

The hand must yield as soon as the horse flexes or shortens his stride, as intended. Obviously the hand yields, along with a yielding seat. When the hands and seat yield, the pressure on the horse's sensitive mouth is undone. But contact is not "dropped"! The gradual undoing of pressure, however, must be faster than was its building. Let us compare this action to that of a rubber band: Pulling a rubber band to a gradual stretch is slower than releasing it to a relaxed connection. When yielding, the rein should never be dropped, never "emptied," never slacking on an advanced horse that takes steady contact. If you do it correctly, the horse will "take your hand" and will not want to release it. Though not pulling on it, he will gently "hold hands with you" and eagerly anticipate this pleasurable contact as part of the harmony that is reestablished. On a young horse, however, contact may periodically slacken to indicate by dramatic yielding approval and to confirm that he can remain longitudinally flexed without using the rider's hands as a "fifth leg" to lean on.

A driving hand is one that "opens," giving the horse an opportunity to stretch his neck and head forward, and as a reward of stretching, seek the bit again. The rein never slackens visibly. However, the horse has momentarily no feel of your hand. Since he needs to "hold hands with you," he will stretch forward to meet your hand. A rider with good hands who creates a good mouth on the horse will always have him eager to step forward to meet his trusted hands. Thus is the horse invited by the hands to move ahead. This, as always, must be coordinated with leg and seat aids saying the same thing: "the door is open, go ahead through it and you will meet me there!"

Reins can be used in three basic positions: direct, indirect and leading. In your imagination hold both reins correctly contacting the horse's mouth at equal distance from it: fists properly placed, close to one another, knuckles almost touching, equidistant from the crest of the horse's neck, and a little higher than his coat. When the hand's position is correct, its uppermost point is the first joint of the thumb. The rein is fixed between this crooked thumb and the second joint of the forefinger. While the rest of the fingers are all bent closed and wrapped around the reins, they remain supple in order to participate in the spring-tension activities of the hand. The wrists are slightly bent inward, rendering the top of the hand a flat continuation of the lower arm. Thus the hand and fingers are turned supple inward, the nails facing your chest.

For a direct rein the basic position of the hand, described above, is maintained. If it contracts backward, the imaginary continuation of the reins would pierce your waist at your belt. The direct rein then acts directly backward, pressing against the horse's mouth. Its effect, when coordinated with the small of your back is to slow down the motion of the horse's head in its forward progression. When sustained, this direct rein action creates a full halt, halting the horse's head while the hindlegs conclude by driving the rest of his body under the center of gravity.

When direct reins are used temporarily and are yielded before the horse comes to a full halt, we have performed a half halt. Half halting is the instrument of longitudinal balancing. It asks the horse to slow down his front end to wait the arrival of the hind end with all its loco-motion, creating the resultant ideal balance. Half halts must be very frequently performed on young horses until such time that they are willing and capable of balancing themselves. From then on half halts are employed only as preparations before any transition from movement to movement. Full halts are used only to halt the horse, and pressure is released only at the time the horse halts fully, four square.

The indirect rein occurs when you so turn your lower arm, and there-fore your wrist, that your nails are upward, though not quite horizontal. With that position the indirect rein is brought against the horse's neck. The imaginary continuation of this rein would pierce your body through the opposite breast. Care must be taken that the indirect hand should never cross over the crest of the horse's neck! While the direct rein can be used simultaneously on both sides of the horse, involving both hands the same way, the indirect hand is always used only on one side.

While the direct rein serves purposes of longitudinal bending by either totally halting or partially slowing down the horse's front end, the pur-pose of an indirect hand is always lateral bending. The indirect rein is relatively passive, should never restrict the horse's impulsion, and while it may yield, should never actually pull in the direction of the opposite breast to which it merely points. It is a passive rein, indicating to the horse the degree of lateral bending expected of him. The indirect rein must always be held against a firmly flexed opposite rein, which will be either in direct or in lead position. If the opposite rein is dropped, the indirect rein becomes meaningless, for without a point of reference against which to function it will be ineffective. While the direct rein acts always as a direct opposition to the movement of the hindleg on the same side, the indirect rein, by never being pulled backward, should never hinder the hindleg's action on the same side.

The inside rein must be always indirect when the horse is laterally bent. Thus, with the exception of halt, rein-back, walking and trotting on a straight line, the indirect rein is used. Even when riding simply through the four corners of an arena, indirect use of the inside rein must come into play. On the straight sides of the arena, however, direct rein is resumed on the inside to create parallel aiding.

The leading rein occurs when you turn your lower arm and wrist so that your nails will face somewhat down toward the ground. This will take the rein away from the horse's neck and will make it point toward your thigh. The leading rein, just like the indirect one, will be used only on one side at the time, against the point of reference that the opposite rein must provide. The opposite rein might be either direct or indirect, depending on the exercise.

This rein position is often useful on young, green horses. Its use diminishes as the horse advances in his understanding of boot and weight aids. The leading rein enables us to lead horses along any line they would naturally move away from should they continue to pursue the course on which their laterally bent bodies are positioned. Thus we may use the leading rein to lead a horse on multitracks. In these movements the horse is not following with his hindlegs the footprints of the front legs. Indeed, with his hindlegs he moves on different, though parallel, tracks with those of the forelegs. In such instances one of the reins, the one indicating the direction of progression, can be rendered a leading rein (at least periodically).

While the direct rein can take the greatest liberty in restricting the horse's forward advancement, the leading rein may take some liberty to do so, leaving the indirect rein as the one forbidden to hinder forward advancement. The lead rein is the one of the three positions most commonly interchanged with either indirect or direct rein. It is one that may rhythmically oscillate back to either direct or indirect rein, depending on need. In short, the lead rein is rarely sustained for a long time, even if the movement that it leads is being sustained.

The position of hand and wrist has been explained for direct, indirect, and lead reins, with the aiding image of "nails in" (close to perpendicular), "nails up," and "nails down," correspondingly. In actuality, however, I do not recommend the twisting of the lower arm into these positions, creating the nail positions as described above! The reason for this is that twisting the wrists into those positions (1) is much too visible, (2) is sometimes disruptive at the horse's mouth, (3) creates rigidly locked hands losing their softness and ability to act as shock-absorbing tension springs, (4) cannot accommodate the carrying of a riding crop.

Therefore, I propose you use the above descriptions to understand where the reins should be in each position, and then proceed to put them there, not by virtue of twisted lower arms, but by moving in and out of your lower arm from the elbow relatively to the horse's neck. If you do that, and you should while riding, you will get the leading rein by lowering your lower arm toward your thigh, and sweeping with it sideways away from the horse's neck toward the direction in which you want to move him. For direct rein keep your arms in basic position, equidistant from the horse's neck. Do not allow the reins to constantly touch his neck and have them point toward your waist. For indirect rein elevate your lower arm until the rein points toward your opposite breast. As the horse advances, these aids are so refined that they become invisible, and the most tender action at the fingers and wrists will create the desired effect. At any rate, the carrying of a riding whip will remain possible even if your aids must be strong enough to be visible. Stiffness in the lower arms certainly will not occur if you create these positions from the elbow joints.

16
Equestrian Clothing and Accessories

Equestrian clothing and accessories can be easily acquired. Much is written and illustrated about proper attire and accessories, and I certainly do not want to add my catalogue to it. However, I can think of some comments that in addition to acquiring proper equipment, may be of some use.

When riding dressage, which is a daily task even on a jumper, and when working over Cavaletti exercises and low jumps, I advise the use of two riding whips one on each side. These whips should be identical. Their length should be about four feet, certainly long enough to reach with ease the horse's sides, behind the boots. Obviously we ride with two legs put in two boots, and when necessary or required with two spurs attached to the boots. Since both the horse and we have two equally important sides, we must not diminish the ability to communicate with each other on one side! Riding with one whip is not only illogical, but it may also be disturbing when the whip is changed over from hand to hand.

In riding, any disturbance, unnecessary and illogical movements, must be eliminated. Furthermore, the use of a whip is only logical when it is instant and used on the side the horse needs this aid. To take time changing the whip to the other side on which it was necessary a minute ago, ruins the whole usefulness. Exception should be made at the time of higher jumping. Then the whip is reserved to quick aiding, usually punishment. A riding crop is shorter, firmer than a training whip, and there should be only one used. Even that is often cumbersome in the quick sport of higher jumping. However, for other than higher jumping, for usual daily work, only two, totally identical, long whips will do the logical job of aiding when it is necessary and where it is understandable.

Ride as much as possible in proper competition attire. It is a grave mistake to introduce new attire and equipment either on horse or on rider just for competition. People who have special competition boots, kept shiny and rigid in a closet, are making a grave mistake. Strange saddles, reserved just for competition, will be most upsetting when things should go best. Let me emphasize that competition coats should be worn as much as the weather permits it. Do not surprise yourself with your tight jacket on the day of competition.

Gloves are required for dressage competition, and at other times wearing them is necessitated by cool weather. Therefore, learn to wear them all the time! Feeling in your hands is very important. It must be cultivated and standardized. Not only is it foolish to switch from bare hands to wearing of gloves, but to switch from a thicker, stiffer, to a thinner, softer glove. Wear the same kind of gloves all the time when riding. That will keep your hands constantly in feeling and civilized looking.

When jumping, always ride in a helmet. Otherwise make sure you wear something that will not allow your hair to disturb you. In general, have clothing and accessories so comfortable that they should no more distract your attention from riding than your own skin does.

Spurs are aids of refinement. They should be used only when the horse has been fully trained to understand leg aids sensitively. They are instruments of "whispering" intimacy rather than equipment for torture. In competition spurs are required only when the horse is shown in full bridle. They are to counteract the possible restrictive effect of the full bridle. Both bridle and spurs should be used only on an advanced horse. They denote a level of sensitivity on which those implements are necessary. Both, spurs and full bridle, are the privilege of advanced and sensitive riders. Do not tamper with spurs on a young horse, regardless how phlegmatic he is. Use the whip to supplement your legs, but never dull a horse or make him rigid by carving him up with spurs.

Spurs, when called for, should be dull and short. They are never to be instruments of pain. They are as short as possible by your relative leg position to the horse's sides. If you are a long-legged person on a narrow little horse, you will need longer spurs to reach him properly. A shorter rider on a thick, large horse can use a shorter spur. But make sure they are dull, and as seldom used as possible.

17
The Riding Tack

The riding tack for the horse must be perfectly suitable for the task and perfectly fitting to the horse. Again, instead of repeating much that has already been well written elsewhere, let me limit my comments to areas that need emphasizing. There should be individual headgear for each horse you ride. Ideally, there could be separate saddles for each horse too. But that is less important than to have individualized headgear. It is of great importance that the horse's headgear fits him correctly. It must be adjusted properly for comfort. Should there be any failure to do so, progress may be halted just because of ill-adjusted, therefore irritating or painful, headgear. Both for purposes of correct and consistent adjustment, and for reasons of health, the horse should receive only his private equipment.

Horses are very conservative in the sense of having a low tolerance level for any change in their environment. Sensitive horses do not eat or drink well in strange stables, and feel the effect of any travel or other change for a long time. They also notice changes in their equipment and will respond to them negatively.

Young horses and jumpers should learn to respond well to the lightest of reins. They need to move on a simple snaffle bit. Make the effect of that bit as light as possible. The thicker the bit the lighter its effects are in the mouth. By all means, try the thickest bits possible, and spend some time succeeding with them. Bits should be jointed in the middle to increase their lightness of effect.

After the leader straps are adjusted on the headgear, cut off any excess length. Not only must the rider always be properly groomed, but the horse's tack must be immaculately clean at all times. Dirty gear creates health hazards, can cause injury, and certainly shows total disrespect toward the horse. The purpose of the saddle is to communicate the rider's seat to the horse's back. Therefore, a good saddle is shaped on top as a mould of the rider's bottom. A good saddle is shaped on the bottom as the contour of the horse's back. Ideally, a saddle should be custom-made to fit the rider exactly throughout its top line and surface, and to follow the shape of the horse's back throughout its bottom surface where it rests on the horse. It is more important for a saddle to fit the rider on the top. The saddle will still be usable on all the horses this same rider rides. Horse's backs are more generalized than are rider's bottoms.

Since the primary concern of dressage and jumping are balance and harmony with the horse, it is indispensable to the task to have a saddle that allows for balance and harmony. The greatest rider in the world, sitting on the most efficiently schooled horse, will fail to harmonize with him if the saddle is incorrect. There is nothing that can substitute for a proper saddle. There is no chance of progress without one. No rider can be taught correct balance, proper seat position, and feeling without a proper saddle. No horse is capable of balancing under the rider and proceeding to shift his center of gravity backward as desired without a correct saddle communicating the rider's seat to him. Lack of a correct saddle immediately forestalls correct equestrian results. No more could a rider accomplish anything on a horse without a proper saddle than could a skier performing in a pair of tennis shoes.

The best saddles are custom-made by a knowledgeable saddlemaker who will study your contour and create a perfectly fitting saddle. However, here are some guidelines as to what you ought to have, in general terms:

Your saddle should be as narrow as possible to accommodate the narrow, natural fall of your legs down both sides of the horse. As you know, your legs come straight upward to a narrow point at the pelvic area. The saddle must peak into the pelvic area and slope directly and straight down on both sides to accommodate that shape. Since the horse's back is roundish and wide, the saddle must have its ridge rather high elevated above his backbone in order to allow its slopes to be straight and direct downward. A wide-topped, roundish saddle puts you away from your horse. For correct contact your legs should fall down directly almost as if you were standing with your legs spread.

The side flaps of the saddle must be thin and soft. They should never catch the top of your boots. They must be short enough to encourage the greatest possible area of contact with the horse's sides. As riding dressage is done mostly by sitting in the saddle rather than posting, minimum knee guarding is desired, and the saddle should not bulge unnecessarily forward in front of the knees. The knees should rest comfortably in front of the stirrup leaders.

The saddle should be as short as possible, while comfortably containing your hip area. There should never be excess space left to navigate on back and forth. A short saddle will ensure the rider's seat remaining in one spot, the right spot at all times.

The deepest point of the saddle should be as forward as possible. There should be, indeed, a rather deep ditch for the deep point. The saddle should never be flat. It should be rather acutely built up in the back to insure the seat remaining well in the front and in the deepest spot.

Riders who cannot advance after a while might find it surprising that they can advance rapidly in a good saddle. Restless, wobbly, insecure, stiff, gripping seats turn often into the finest, most effective seat when put into a suitable saddle.

18
The Riding Area and Grounds

The riding area and grounds largely determine the possibilities and level of training. They must be suitable, or achievement cannot be expected! It is difficult to describe an ideal equestrian center, for it can only be ideal in terms of need in that area, and in terms of land and capital available. However, one could consider something idealistic and then make compromises to suit one's needs and financial possibilities. Certainly, talking about an equestrian center is worth our while, for so many riding places exist that are incorrectly conceived, though the same amount of capital with more know-how would have produced a more admirable result.

An equestrian center should provide facilities for the following activities: riding instruction and horse training, including instructional theory and riding and horse training; horse shows and examinations for riders and horses; and breeding.

Theoretical equestrian intsruction is indispensable. Riding is a sport that is also an art form based on sound theoretical knowledge. No one can ride successfully without knowing the goals and theory of riding, the nature and physique of the horse. All equestrians must know the theory of riding before practicing it. They must know the possibilities of riding, the correct use of aids, and the logical sequence of gymnastics. They must know the use of particular exercises, and the possible combination of them. Riders must learn about proper health care and diet of horses, about proper modes of transportation. They also must know how to organize horse shows, build jumping courses, and judge shows. They must know so much that a whole library of books must be read, lectures attended, discussions going on all the time. Films must be watched, discussed, and evaluated. Other riders must be watched, judged, instructed. There is in fact so much to know in the equestrian field that one cannot finish learning in a lifetime. Riding means perpetual learning. The riding academy or equestrian center must provide for its correct foundations, much like high schools and universities merely provide intensified, systematic programs of learning on which lifelong learning is based.

In each equestrian center there should be an instructional center, a facility for theoretical learning. Students should be required to study text books, discuss them, and pass examinations based on their contents. Students be encouraged to live in the equestrian center, and exchange ideas with each other and with their instructors all the time, even informally. There should be a classroom where good charts on the horse's physique are available, his skeleton, his muscular structure, his major physical points and outlines.

A whole new equestrian vocabulary has to be taught. Not only is it necessary to know the horse's physique and function of his body, but also know the terminology of riding instruction and judging. There should be blackboards. Other dynamic systems of riding should be denoted in permanent painting on boards. Chalk drawings can be added to these outlines by the instructors. There should be film and slide projectors, and a screen to observe them. There should be a film library, a book library, and subscriptions to current magazines and journals. There should be picture files. These materials should encompass all possible equestrian activities from breeding to show jumping, from health care to saddlery. Equestrian life is a syndrome composed of many elements, none of which is comprehensible without a sufficient overview of the whole.

In the instructional center there should be another large board on which the map of the entire facility is shown. From time to time designs of training and competitive courses can be chalked into this permanent map. New designs, expansions, and planting should be noted on this board also.

Mock horses, saddles, bridles, and other equipment should be part of the instructional center to facilitate learning of positions and techniques away from the horse, who should be relieved of functions as a living chair, or trial-and-error kit. Respect for the horse must saturate equestrians, and even small gestures and attitudes must consistently reinforce this ideology.

Riding and horse training need ample space. Ideally, there should be large areas for cross-country rides. While these must not necessarily be owned by the equestrian center, some use of public or private properties should be secured for open distance riding. Each horse needs a foundation, as near as possible approximating his natural environment, created in the outdoors, roaming through large spaces. Later, when the horse is specialized for purposes of higher attainments, cross-country rides should continue about once a week. This will refresh the horse, break the monotony of his working routine, invest him with new strength and vigor, and maintain desirable muscle strength and stamina. It will add to his appetite and to his zest for working.

The riding area or arenas on one's own property should be surrounded entirely by a great canter ring. The entire perimeter of any riding area, however large or small, should be a continuous wide bend for distance cantering and general " forward" work. Horses should be warmed up on this path and ridden forward on it daily. "Lung work" should be done on it. For speed work or any work that needs timing the great canter circle is indispensable. Jumps can be positioned on it periodically for speed jumping and for building of courage and stamina. Dressage horses also need forward, straight stretches. The best piaffes and passages can be taught and exercised on these rings, for they invite the horse to move freely forward, and offer great impulsion.

Within the canter ring the various arenas should be built and positioned. It is wise to have at least two properly sized dressage courts, with permanent lettering. One may be sand and the other lawn to facilitate training on each footing. Both footings occur in competition. One of the arenas may serve for competition, while the other remains for warming up. Or there may be so many dressage entries at a competition that two sets of judges must be engaged, and two arenas busy for the testing of riders. During everyday work periods a minimum of two dressage courts is necessary for concentrated, sophisticated work.

It is wise to position these dressage arenas in opposite lettering. In one arena letter A should be at the same end where in the other arena letter C is shown. Many riders memorize dressage tests according to trees and other landmarks on their training ground. When away in competition they lose track of their program, which they never learned to ride when "turned around." Various influences of sun, wind, etc. must be experienced by riding in dressage courts, positioned differently in their relative environment.

There should be also at least two different jumping arenas. One should have equipment for Cavaletti and other rhythm work spread all around it. This arena is good for daily gymnasticizing of the horses. During competition this same arena can be used for warming up horses.

The other arena should be left for big jumps, and at times of shows for stadium jumping competition. This arena should have at least one permanent bank, but preferably more, also, a permanent water ditch, rather wide. It should also have a permanent, deep dry ditch. In the center of this jumping arena it is advisable to position permanently, or even "dig in" the so-called star jumping combination. This is indispensable for correct jumper's training, and excellently functional as part of a competition course.

This "star combination" of jumps is indispensable in training exercises for jumpers. It is excellent when included in competition courses. At about the center of the arena you should build a double jump. Position it so that during competition the spectators can see it from the side, since combinations, indeed, are of special interest. Then build four more jumps that are each positioned at forty-five degree angles to the wings of both units constituting the double jump. Make these jumps, a total of six fences, vastly different from one another in nature, character, and looks. Some should be in natural colors, some brightly painted. Some should be vertical jumps, while others spread jumps. During competition you should be able to vary their height and width.

Jumpers could be moved around this star combination on a large circle at the trot or the canter. When the horse is calm, composed, and yielding to the aids, the rider can turn him to one of these jumps from a relatively short distance. These six jumps can provide interesting tasks when combined into a continuous course in a variety of ways. During training one can jump them when the horse is in ideal readiness. One can also plan a course of successive jumps without trying to jump the fences one right after the other. Just jump them when the rider and horse are in ideal condition to negotiate these jumps.

Ideally there should be permanently constructed booths for the dressage judges. They should provide deep shading for restful observation during long competition hours. They should protect the judges and their secretaries from wind. Care should be taken that no part of the construction will obstruct the full view of the dressage court.

There should be a permanent score board for competition results, also another board at the warm-up arena for pegging courses on and for displaying the order of riders in competition.

There should be some provision made for spectator comfort. Not only during competition, but during training days also there may be relatives, friends, or interested colleagues watching. There should be permanent viewing facilities, such as bleachers. They should be shaded, and accommodate as many people as hoped for during large competitions. Rest rooms and parking facilities are also obviously needed.

Riding should be a pleasure for the equestrian, for the horse, and for the spectators. Therefore the aesthetic appearance of an equestrian center is of utmost importance. The whole art form of riding is concerned with beauty. Daily work and performance naturally improve in beautiful environments. Improved function is, obviously, the result of the stimulus that only beauty can provide. Inspiration is a great part of good riding, and beautiful terrain to ride on surely contributes to success.

Therefore I strongly recommend that all permanent structures should possess beauty; that the whole arrangement of an equestrian center be concerned with good proportions and fine architecture. I urge the building of beautiful jumps. But most important of all, fill the property with plants. An equestrian center should appear to be set in the midst of a great park. Shade is pleasant for all concerned. Shrubs, flowers, and trees also protect from wind, and hold the carefully prepared soil on the premises. Planting reduces dust flying during the hot summer days, and encourages better drainage during rainy seasons. In spite of the multitudes of utilitarian functions that plants supply, their greatest utility remains in their provision of beauty. Plant trees and shrubs to serve as wings to the permanently positioned jumps. Make green islands around jumps. Allow climbing plants to cover with blossoms and greenery the wooden wings of jumps. Plant shrubs that can be clipped to serve as parts of a jump or as a take-off line for a jump. Create flower beds. Turn the nonriding areas of your property into a lush green blooming park area. It will attract people. One word of caution: Oleanders are poisonous to horses. Horses should never nibble on oleander bushes. Since they are very easy to grow in warmer, dryer states in the United States, they offer a great temptation for planting. They are indeed beautiful and fast growing, without substantial care. However, omit them from your equestrian center.

Near the stable areas there should be baths for watering horses' legs. Horses' legs, even when healthy, benefit from regular water therapy. After work as well as on resting days, horses should stand an hour in water. The baths should be so constructed that the horse could walk into them on a gradual ramp. Neither the ramp nor the bottom of the bath should be slippery. Water should reach as high as possible up the legs without ever touching the horse's body. Therefore water should not reach the chest or belly! In these legs baths, on hot days, horses can be washed too.

There should also be grooming paddocks. Horses must be cross-tied to posts and be groomed on a dry, clear footing that can easily be swept up with a push broom. Cleanliness is probably the most important compliment to an equestrian center. Both, the love for the horse, for whom the whole establishment exists, and protection of the investment, demand outstanding cleanliness. That should saturate all aspects of the riding establishment. All riding areas, paddocks, and areas where horses may move, must be picked clean of rocks, nails, boards, and must in general look clean. As a matter of fact, areas where horses move must be groomed. They must be level, raked, clean of manure. Wherever possible areas should be frequently swept. Stables and stalls must be cleaned of manure and used up bedding and other discarded materials. Horses must be groomed, ideally twice a day, once before, and once after work. Saddles and other tack must be cleaned daily, once a month thoroughly. Everything should be spotlessly kept.

I hope it is clearly understood that great equestrian achievement is pieced together by small, daily acts. Among them one must place in an important position cleanliness of both horses and equipment. Correct grooming of the entire horse is important. So is correct feeding, done on schedule, and according to careful study of needs.

An equestrian center should be quiet. We must never underestimate the harm done to the human nervous system by noise pollution. Even in a tranquil country environment, noises from cars, airplanes, household machinery, intrude on our nervous system. Horses have far keener hearing than we do. Their tranquility must very much be guarded, and permanent quiet insured. They can neither rest nor work when there are noises. They cannot rationalize noises like humans can, and will react to them instinctively. Instinct demands horses to be alert, even upset when noises are present. Therefore never establish an equestrian center near major highways where the hissing of cars, thundering of trucks, provide a never-ending promenade of noises. Do not place it within earshot of noisy railroads.

While you think of the obvious noise-producing machines and decide to avoid them, do not forget people. I may have exaggerated sentiments in regard to horses, but I remain continuously shocked how noisily riders behave around horses. Forbid that! Rider education entails a great deal more than being limited to riding a horse. It is incredible that owners of riding establishments, and coaches, should omit from their education the value of quiet around horses. Riders tally-ho-ing around stables, shrieking their latest gossip from box to box, cussing at their horses while grooming them, certainly are exhibiting unethical behavior, unbecoming to equestrians. They certainly constitute unnecessary disturbances to the great number of horses that are alarmed by the noises. Equestrians talk little, and then quietly, around horses. They behave quietly, and with calm movements around horses. These attitudes must be cultivated in equestrian centers and enforced for the sake of horses who are our central concern.

Horses should be well cooled off before taken back to their stall. To save time and energy, a riding establishment may want to install a cooling mechanism called a hot walker, to which horses that worked can be attached. They can be walked cool without people's assistance on hot-walkers.

Longeing is a very important part of training a horse, and an equally important part of creating a skillful rider. There should be, therefore, a permanent longeing arena in each serious equestrian center. When the horse is being longed he moves in a circle that has a radius equal to the length of the longeing line that is held by an instructor in the center. This circle, on which the horse moves, should be surrounded by a circular plank fence. The fence, just like any railing of a riding arena, should slant outward to allow for greater room higher up. The horse's bulky body, on him the rider and his legs, move farther out than the horse's legs on the ground. So, the bottom of arena walls should be outside the horse's footprints, while the top line of the fence should lean outward to accommodate a rider's legs.

Depending on goals for which an equestrian center is built, many more special facilities could be recommended. Space does not allow, however, greater expansion on this subject here. I merely feel that certain things are extremely necessary for the correct functioning of riding centers, and they are often missing from many that I have visited. Therefore, I deem some guidance in this matter may be useful.

19
Riding Instruction

Riding instruction can be divided into two different phases, according to need. The need is determined by the participants of an instructional situation: the rider, the horse, and the instructor.

First, the object of instruction is the novice or beginning rider. Ideally, he should be riding a well-schooled horse. His instructor must proceed to teach him riding as a skill. The goal of instruction at this stage, then, is to impart the craftsmanship of riding to the rider. The rider is the only pupil; both the horse and the instructor are teachers.

This phase of instruction is often called *equitation*. The rider is expected to acquire (1) balance on the horse, which will enable him to develop (2) an independent seat that is relaxed and not gripping anywhere in order to stay on the horse. Finally, the balanced, independent seat will allow the rider to learn (3) correct communications with the horse—in other words, the aiding system. When this triple aim is accomplished, a skilled rider is created who knows the craftsmanship of riding.

While the above outlined physical development takes place, simultaneously an academic and character development must also be fostered. There can be no outstanding riding without extensive academic knowledge, nor can there be any success without a suitable character development. The instructor must see to it that academic reading is done by the pupil, and offer theoretical instruction and opportunities for discussion. Such instruction will result in a skilled, independent rider who may proceed to the second stage of instruction.

In the second stage of instruction the object of effort will be the horse. Once the rider is properly skilled in the technique of riding, is theoretically prepared, and knowledgeable, he can begin to school horses. Now the goal of instruction is to advance a horse, and as he improves, show him in various stages of competition. As a consequence, both rider and

Young riders should learn balanced and independent seat on the longe line. The instructor controls the horse from the center, giving an opportunity to the young rider to fully relax in the saddle. TOP: *The young rider is lifted to the saddle to begin his longeing lesson in Verden, Germany.* BOTTOM: *A large competition audience admires the vaulting exhibition of correctly started, perfectly balanced and supple young riders in northern Germany.*

instructor are now teachers, and the horse is the pupil.

In this second stage the instructor becomes a coach who co-instructs the horse with the rider. Ideally, the rider's skills should need no more correcting. Equitation, at best, should need no more attention. However, sometimes certain bodily attitudes and uses may be suggested or corrected. After all, the first stage of the rider's instruction could not impart all the more sophisticated aids that now may come into use as the rider is advancing.

A good coach will inspire confidence in the rider, will consult the rider as to what he feels, perceives, on his horse. He will seek the rider's explanations of feelings before offering his impressions. In other words a good coach must promote the rider's independence, which comes only through increased sensitization of the rider. A good coach should never "hang onto his job" by insisting on keeping his rider dependent. He should never degrade himself to the level of a crutch on whom the rider will lean for feelings and for dictation of tyrannical dogmas. Do remember that the most important aspect of this stage of riding is that the rider and instructor are co-educators of the horse.

A good coach will: (1) *perceive* all problems as they arise, and will perceive problems correctly; (2) *know* instantly all possible and probable remedies to the problems arising, the hierarchy of effectiveness of the various possible remedies, how to communicate effectively, quickly, and clearly about the problem and its correction; (3) *accomplish* prevention of problems by correct and systematic development of the horse, steady progress of the horse, correct and permanent eradication of problems as they arise.

The coach, therefore, must be outstandingly prepared in the theory of riding. He must have a firm academic background that he can impart to his rider too. He also must be an accomplished rider who can succeed with reasonable demands on the horse-pupil when his less-experienced rider should fail to do so. He should be able to prove a point by demonstrating it. Most important, however, he should be an accomplished rider for two reasons: (1) to acquire the trust and respect of the rider, and (2) to be able to "feel" the horse as if he were to ride it, while watching and coaching from the ground.

By now it must be obvious that there are more instructors prepared to teach a rider equitation than to coach. There are few good coaches possessing both the academic knowledge and practical experience to help a rider develop a horse.

Acquisition of riding skills is preliminary to independent riding. Independent riding eventually leads to artistry. It is not true that all independent riders, all those more or less capable of developing horses, are all artistic riders. However, some accomplished riders may reach the stage of artistry. I think it is a very special boon if a rider has the good luck to be inspired by a coach who is an artist in horsemanship.

In riding, the same creative attributes and principles are applicable as in the fine arts. An artistic rider will base his artistry on perfection of craftsmanship. He will be well versed in the academic principles of his art. Yet, he will take flight from these foundations and add to them his unique insight. His creativity will be manifest and displayed in his daily dressaging, and will permeate his performances. He will add refinement relevant to his horse and the particular task. He will contribute novelties to the general body of existing academic knowledge. He will introduce novelty and polish in his riding, which is not commonly seen. All this will not come about by alteration of the general principles of riding that crystallized through two thousand years of application and success. However, the artistic rider will constantly invent new combinations of the existing methods, materials, and principles, thus creating curiously suitable syndromes that will particularly enhance his horse's brilliance in performance.

An artistic rider has usually an outstandingly clear conception of his goals and of the best possible way to attain them. He has a "vision" that he can eventually recreate. His sensitivity to both, horse and task to be achieved, is keener than that of an average rider. He can also individualize and diversify from traditional generalizations with greater insight than could an average rider.

Riders always need an instructor. While acquiring their skills they need daily, intense instruction. Their independence is severely curtailed by their lack of knowledge. They often are so dependent on an instructor that they are actually being longed by one. They are not even permitted to steer the horse or regulate his paces at first. Later dependence is lessened, but due to constant necessity of correcting, and constant repetitions on the use of correct aids, they are still held in a highly dependent position.

As a skilled rider will switch to being coached rather than instructed, he will have to become, even encouraged, to act independently, using as the most reliable guidance his own perceptions and feelings. Should the rider be so talented as to emerge as an artist, he will continue to need the support of a coach. A rider's feelings should constantly be verified from the ground. A good coach, being an artist himself, with great academic knowledge and much expensive behind him, remains indispensable throughout the competition career of even the most artistic rider. Not only is the eye of the coach indispensable, but so is his inspiration, guidance, and physical help from the ground. Especially in jumping, a man on the ground is necessary to set up obstacles and be there in case of an emergency. In dressage, the "eye" on the ground can assume the position of an evaluator, a judge, and help the rider accomplish a desired ideal.

While the rider is still in the first stage of his learning, still acquiring the skills of the art, he needs intense theoretical instruction. This should be, ideally, formal sessions of instruction. The rider should read recommended literature. He should look at photographs and films, and discuss them with his instructor. He should watch competitions, especially the best riders. He should constantly try to "ride along" with those whom he watches, "feel" what they are doing, then continue to discuss. Good students of this art form will be easily recognizable by their insaturable curiosity, quest, and questioning. Even later, when the rider has become independent, theoretical discussions should continue. He should keep up to date with current equestrian literature after having read all the important literature of the past. He should now intensify his visual studies that should include photographs and films of his own riding. He should now not only watch others compete, but expose himself to the eye of judges. Each judge's evaluation should serve as instructional guidance, and be thoroughly discussed with his regular coach. He should seek to attend "clinics" by other, but good, coaches to listen to diversified insights concerning his efforts and problems. All competition should be perceived as learning experience. Failures and successes should be learned from and used as inspiration for further improvement.

Accomplished, independent riders should begin to watch fellow competitors with a degree of expertise. An expert is one who has achieved the highest level of cognitive function, that of evaluation. Thus, the rider should write "protocols" of other riders' performances. He should improve his ability to observe, evaluate, and then express in concise terms that which he perceived. He can dictate his perceptions into a tape recorder or write them down. Both will be "protocols" and serve the desired purpose. As the rider improves the degree of his expertise, he will have to improve his ability to be an instructor and judge. He certainly will have to intensify his self-instruction.

A good riding instructor must possess the attributes of an outstanding educator. He must have full command of his subject matter, must be patient, and show understanding and willingness to help. He should communicate clearly and concisely. An instructor should invite questioning, and welcome the contesting of his ideas. He must be highly creative and inventive, must fully respect his pupils, be it horse or rider. His enthusiasm should never show want, his encouragement never slack. He should have clear goals, and work every day with a particular purpose in mind. Without overall goals, and within that framework, daily aims, there can be no meaningful instruction. All details must add up to serving the basic goals that determine the general direction of work. Since the skilled rider is also a teacher, the educator of his horse, he must develop also the properties of an educator.

Ideally, a riding instructor should work with only one pupil at a time. In this complex art full instructional attention is imperative. Obviously, when longeing a student, it is physically impossible to have more than one on the longe tape. However, later, when riders are capable of steering their horses and can work semi-independently, riding classes may be formed to save time and energy. If such classes must be formed the number of participants should not exceed twelve, and they should be all more or less on the same level of craftsmanship. It is rather important that pupils working in groups should be divided into groups according to levels of knowledge. Otherwise one or two slacking pupils will demand the instructors attention, to the detriment of other riders.

Ideally, accomplished riders should also work alone with the instructor. Group sessions, however, often become necessary. On an advanced level riders can benefit from weekend clinics, offered by guest instructors. Those still in the equitation stage of instruction cannot fully benefit from clinics. However, when accomplished riders are grouped together for instruction it is advisable to allow them to work independently, spread throughout the arena, rather than work in a class under commands. The instructor then observes the independently riding equestrians, and offers comments to those who need it at the time. Periodically some of them may be summoned to the instructor for discussion, and then allowed to proceed according to advice. Special problems can be worked out with individual riders while the others continue to work their horses independently.

When riding in groups under instruction, comments made to one rider may be invaluable to all the rest of the riders. Pupils should listen eagerly for comments offered to anyone in class, for those are relevant to all riders, if not now, then possibly at later times, or on other horses.

When instructing a class of riders the instructor should commence the session by asking the riders to line up side by side on their horses, and face him. He can then greet the riders, and if necessary offer general comments as to the procedures he expects to follow, and describe some goals for that day. Tasks must be made clear to riders all the time. Then the instructor should step up to each rider and inspect his horse and equipment. Both horse and equipment should be meticulously clean. Correct grooming must be insisted upon, and where short of proper standards, future improvements must be insisted upon. Equipment should be corrected as to fit horse and rider perfectly, stirrup length adjusted, straps on head stall adjusted, and unused lengths of leader cut off. As the inspection proceeds riders should report to the instructor about the condition of their horse. They can make special requests. Riders may mention any new problems that may have arisen since the last lesson. They should mention any diseases or weaknesses. In short, report concisely and briefly anything that may be relevant in shaping the daily work. After inspection each rider is dismissed from the line-up and is to proceed limbering up his horse for work.

During riding the equestrian should never talk. Rather, he must at all times be fully absorbed in his task of riding. He ought to remain in uninterrupted communication with his horse. Should any serious question ever arise, the rider should walk, on a long rein, to the center of the arena, and wait for the instructor's attention, then explain and discuss the matter on his mind. Riders may never converse among each other, may never answer back an instructor during riding.

During good instruction praises and positive comments are just as important as scolding ones. Since it is presumed that the rider seeks instruction because he needs it, we cannot expect to hear mostly praises from the instructor. If the rider would be so good as to warrant only praise and admiration, he would not be in need of instruction. However, whenever a chance is offered, the instructor must reward with praise. It is important that the good moments be pointed out. Otherwise the rider cannot develop a correct feeling for that which is desirable. He must know how it feels when something is good. He must recall what he did to produce the desired outcome. So the good moments must be pointed out and emphasized by the instructor.

It has always been a difficult task to find adequate coaching. As the academies that traditionally and systematically created riding instructors and coaches gradually disappear, the situation is becoming threatening to the very existence of this art form. Even in the days previous to World War II, when many fine academies turned out great numbers of graduates, the truly outstanding instructors were few and far between. Now that much fewer riding academies attract much fewer aspirants, the emergence of great instructors might seem unlikely. As the situation is reaching desperate proportions, I can only hope that some equestrians will be determined to continue, on their own, in the finest of classical riding tradition; that by using all the great text books, by taking advantage of the surviving few great instructors, by competing in front of the best possible judges, and by dedicating their life to the development of many and capable horses, they will emerge someday as the upholders of correct riding tradition. Then they will be able to teach, to coach, to inspire an art, and to judge impartially, with great facility, in the name of the classical principles, without compromise.

20
Viewing and Judging Dressage

Riding in general, and dressage in particular, is a spectator sport. Since the goals of dressage (those being mental and physical balance, suppleness and obedience of the horse) are attained by constant, meaningful and systematic gymnasticizing of the horse, a dressage competition consists of a sequence of exercises that display meaningful gymnastics to be performed by the horse. The rider memorizes the sequence of these gymnastics, called the dressage test. However, riders ought to be reminded not to "ride the test," but rather to "ride the horse" during a show.

Dressage competitions are delightful to watch for anyone who can be inspired by beauty that emerges from seemingly effortless, rhythmic, disciplined, supple, yet powerful and purposeful movements that are exhibited by the horse and rider, who are united into a harmonious, dynamic system of perfectly coordinated motions. The greater the spectator's knowledge of what he sees, the greater his enjoyment will be. That increased knowledge of an art form increases its enjoyment is a well-known principle of art appreciation. It is to be assumed that the judge differs from the general audience in that he is an expert, with knowledge exceeding that of most of the other spectators; that he holds delegated powers to evaluate riders showing, according to his expertise.

The quality of riding in any country, or in any given area, will much depend on the availability of expert judges. Judges have the power to establish the standards of ideal toward which riders will have to work with their coaches. Should these ideals, these standards be false, the entire goal orientation of an area will be toward ill-stated principles. This will inevitably result in compromising, or even losing sight of the great classical principles of dressage.

Riders, their coaches, and the generally interested public will develop the concepts of what is correct and what is wrong by the pronouncement of judges in any area. Good judges foster good riding, and also educate a public whose eyes are being nourished on good riding.

Who Is a Good Dressage Judge?

1. He must be extensively schooled in the theory of classical riding. He must be thoroughly read in the subject matter. He must know the ideals of classical dressage, and be dedicated to upholding them without compromise.

2. He should, ideally, have completed a reputable equestrian academy where academic instruction as well as many hours of daily riding were the regular routine. Failing that, he should have studied under an outstanding riding instructor for a considerable length of time.

3. He should have trained young, green horses successfully to that level of attainment that he is invited to judge. Preferably, he should have successfully competed on the very level he is now to judge.

4. He should have had sufficient diversification of riding experience, having gained routine on hundreds of horses, to be able to "ride along" with the performer throughout the entire program, and thus not only see, but feel the performance.

5. He must be able to perceive a dressage program as an artistically total unit, much like a symphony, rather than perceiving it only in details of exercises, as if hearing only single musical notes without a melody.

6. He should have an untiring ambition to patiently evaluate each and every rider with equal enthusiasm and empathy. He must never tire in maintaining mental concentration and keenness. He should cultivate a great appetite and unquenchable curiosity toward each new rider entering the competition arena. While for him it may be the twentieth, rather primitively performed test he is watching, for the rider in front of him that is the only test, the very one that he prepared for conscientiously. A judge who cannot respect each and every rider and his effort cannot be expected to be equally keen in observing them.

7. He must possess fast and accurate perception. He must be expert enough to deal with multitudes of impressions and in seconds respond to these impressions with an accurate analysis. He certainly must maintain a high level of awareness of all the good things he sees and feels, and not only of the shortcomings and mistakes.

It must be understood, however, that, because of lack of time and lack of space on the evaluation sheets, the judge's comments will necessarily be stingy, yet hopefully concise. These comments are mostly negative, for it is expected of a judge to point out areas in need of improvement. Competition, ideally, should be an educational, not a ribbon-gathering experience. Riders must expect comments that enable them to improve in the future by eliminating shortcomings and correcting mistakes.

Ideally, each judge should dictate into a tape recorder a full monologue of impressions. He should verbalize all his thoughts that occur during the ride. Those, of course, should include positive and negative thoughts that in turn would be recorded on a tape, as they are verbalized spontaneously. The next best thing to a dictation of all the impressions during a ride is a written "protocol" or evaluation that could later be mailed or handed to the rider to be attached to his score sheet. The use of "protocols," either tape recorded and therefore detailed and spontaneous, or written and therefore more considerate, accurate, but less extensive, should greatly improve equestrian standards.

8. Judges must be uncompromisingly ethical, and judge impartially. They must judge only that which is done in the competition arena. Judges must never be influenced by impressions they receive from gossipers and well-wishers. They should not watch with deference the great "stars." They should never judge under the influence of previous memories, be they positive or negative in nature. They should never judge under the influence of what they saw from the corner of their eyes in the warm-up ring.

9. Judges should have studied specifically the techniques of judging. Judging is one of the most difficult endeavors in an equestrian career. Beyond great knowledge, practical and theoretical, beyond natural talents of concentration, observation, perception, sensitivity, enthusiasm, and others, a judge must learn the actual technique of judging. That takes, among other things, a great deal of time, judging with a master judge, and discussing with him afterward all the impressions.

10. Finally, spectators, and of course judges, must cultivate a love of that which is correct. Avoid becoming a person who thrives on the perverted joy of witnessing failure and weakness. Do not thrive on a false sense of security cultivated by demoralizing comments hurled at the riders.

Knowledgeable spectators and judges are distinguishable from others by their attitude of attending shows expecting to be delighted. They should cultivate an attitude of anticipation of the good moments, the highlights, the appearance of beautiful things.

Obviously we would not call anyone an "opera fan" who would go to opera performances anticipating a false note from the soprano, or a break in the tenor's voice when he hits a high note. Opera fans will not typically go to a performance to see the leading lady stumble down a flight of stairs, or to witness the chorus bulldoze away a set of cardboard pyramids. Knowledgeable spectators, preeminently the expert judge, are expected to seek thrills by witnessing perfection rather than thrills that may come by mishaps. The more one is aware of the good in performances, the more knowledge one can claim. For what is knowledge, if not the acquaintance with the ideals? In the equestrian art all that is correct appears beautiful. That beauty, the by-product of correctness, is what is spectacular in this spectator sport.

21
Thoughts about Competition

Competition is a challenge. It serves multiple purposes.

1. Competitions are educational experiences. Riders are given a chance to test the level of perfection they attained during their careful, systematic preparations. They are given a chance to be evaluated by expert judges on expertly designed tests both in jumping and in dressage. They are to learn not only from their own competition experiences, but also by watching other riders who came from distant places and address themselves now to the same task.

2. Competitions offer great stimulus to riders. They help riders formulate their goals and encourage riders to prepare by a certain deadline a certain degree of accomplishment. They afford an opportunity to exchange ideas, either by conversation with fellow competitors, judges, and coaches, or by watching other people's rides, and learn from their techniques and attainments.

3. Competitions offer an opportunity for riders to set precedents, to be displayed to others who can learn from them. It is a show of good and bad from which all participants can and should learn.

4. Competitions offer high level challenges and professionally standardized goals of attainment against which the rider can test his readiness.

Never compete for ribbons. Perform as perfectly as you and your horse are capable of doing. Rather take two poles on a jumping competition, but have a well-planned ride with gentle hands and a relaxed, obedient horse on the rein. Do not display roughness in order to win. In the long run correct riders will succeed. Rough riders who make compromises might succeed once by chance, but they have done irreparable damage to their horse, and that will hinder them later. Never compete on any level for which you are not adequately prepared.

The beauty of a jumping arena during competition.

Aachen's dressage court during competition, showing the judges' booths, secretariat, score board, and good taste in lettering and floral decorations.

Competition without proper preparation and readiness for it is un-ethical. It may inflict injury on horse and rider. It also offends judges and spectators. People never go to shows to see greed exhibited by tor-turing a horse with force and through fear to take a chance at winning ribbons. In competition something good to be shown is expected, and not greed served by riding for chance and luck.

An equestrian who loves and respects his horse and is devoted to the art of riding, rather than being devoted to ribbons, will never overtax his horse. He will never demand of his performances that which he has not adequately prepared. A horse should compete on levels beyond which he can already work during daily sessions. He is to show polish and demonstrate it effortlessly.

A horse should never see his first four-foot obstacle in a jumping competition. If he is shown over four-foot fences in competition, it is to be presumed he can already jump higher without fear and agitation, and with pleasure, zest, and self-confidence.

A horse shown in third-level dressage is presumed to have begun gym-nasticising on fourth-level exercises, that his advance into fourth-level gymnastics is indeed the reason for his being so effortless and supple in a third-level competition ride. Never teach new things in a competition ring. Do not make competition the most taxing and novel of sessions. Competition should be limited to that level of attainment which by now is effortless.

It is hoped that I am describing an ever-shrinking number of com-petitions with an ever-diminishing number of exhibitors who show totally unprepared horses. However, much too often the pictures of such riders emerge: riders whose horses jump out of fear; stiff, resistant, scared horses that cannot understand the inconsistent aids and other disturbances of an ineffective, cruel, and unbalanced rider; horses equipped with mechanical brakes of twisted wire bits, full bridles, stand-ing martingales, who are urged forward by whips beating on them, and sharp spurs carving into their sides with powerful jabs that are coming from a great distance.

Riders who enter a dressage court where it is becoming to show a balanced, supple, and obedient horse, often lack even a balanced seat, and disturb their horses so pathetically that the judge can only hope they will leap out of the court by accident, and thus disqualify.

Competitions are not really won in the competition arena. They are won before, not only by proper preparation of the horse, but by careful attention to all his needs, such as feeding, grooming, safety, health care, and good transportation, which are just as essential to competition suc-cess as is thorough training under a fine coach.

Jumping competitions are not really decided over the obstacles. Much more important, they are decided by what happens before and after each obstacle. They are decided by the careful strategy and planning of the rider. One should never ride twelve separate jumps, but one continuous, intimately interrelated course.

We must keep in mind that great competition successes result from thousands of things done in the past. The nature of the competition determines warming up procedures. However, the general aims of warming up always include the goals of a relaxed, supple, obedient horse moving courageously forward to the slightest of aids. Be it high jumping or dressage, these remain the goals we must pursue during warm-up.

It is important that the horse's forward zest, suppleness, and obedience be established as quickly and with as little expenditure of energy as possible. The better a horse's training has served preparation for the competition, the shorter the time necessary in the actual warm-up will be. A horse that is truly ready for the competition task will limber up in a very short time, and with great conservation of energy. Both horse and rider must be relaxed physically and mentally before a competition. Tensions must be avoided. Unusual and new tasks should not be asked of the horse. Warming-up should be made a very pleasurable experience for the horse.

For jumping competitions warming up should be over combination fences. Ideally, one unit of the combination should be vertical, while the other a spread jump. This combination should be negotiated from both sides, with obviously different techniques. Then each of the units of this combination should be jumped separately, from an angular approach.

Horses need gymnastics on combination jumps, as a preparation for a competition course. They must review their timing and rhythm, and that can best be done over combinations. The jumps must not be high for limbering up. Just before the rider is called into the competition arena, he should jump one smaller, spread jump. Doing that will make the first jump in the competition arena much as if it were the second jump.

When saluting the judge before riding the course is required, it is well to rein-back the horse a few steps and strike into canter from that position. The rein-back will encourage collection, the bending of hindquarters, the "coiling of springs," and will once more check out the horse's obedience, suppleness and forward urge. Then on to the course.

Warming up for dressage should ideally be in two installments. If time permits, the first warm-up should occur several hours before competition. The horse should not spend much energy uselessly. He should be gymnasticized until he is very supple, concentrates obediently to all aids, and is moving forward with great appetite and joy. Then it is time to send him back and be watered, lightly fed, massaged, and groomed.

The second warm-up should be right before competition. Usually fifteen minutes are allotted for the use of the warm-up, holding dressage court, while the preceding performer is in the competition court.

In these last fifteen minutes one can briefly review some of the competition exercises. Never ask for anything new or difficult. Make sure the whole effort is less demanding than on any regular working day. Do not sour, hurt, or fight the horse. Let him compete with spirit.

The distances between units of combination jumps must be carefully measured. The horse's strides, their length and degree of collectedness must be planned for the clean jumping of these combinations. A rider plans each approach to each jump carefully. He plans the angle of the approach. He plans the length of the horse's strides and the degree of his seatedness before take-off. He plans the exact spot of the take-off. He will plan not only how far back his horse will stand back to jump, but also where he will do so relative to the obstacle's center.

Coaches should educate their riders to the perception of jumping courses, and help them create appropriate riding strategy for them. They should also see to it that the decided rising strategy is preeminently demonstrated during the ride. All the education must take place on the training grounds at home, as well as adhered to during competitions. Eventually, as the rider matures through routine, he will grow more and more independent in his ability to correctly assess the logic of his courses, and ride with appropriate plans, with a horse fully under control.

One often wishes that all competitions would be organized for the benefit and pleasure of the participants. Unfortunately, however, there are often inadequate warming-up arenas. Also, there may be inadequate loudspeaker communications. Often there is a mysterious secretiveness about the time each rider will take the competition course. Great delays. Confusing changes in schedule. In other words, the management acts as if no strategy in warming up to and executing a competition course is ever necessary. They seem to act as if the beauty of competition is that results come by chance; that competition ought to show which riders can stay cool in conditions of crisis, rather than which riders can academically plan a fine ride, and prepare for it adequately. All these shortcomings, where they exist, ought to be eliminated.

22
What Is the Kür?

The Kür is a dressage test designed by the rider who will execute it. In my opinion the highest form of dressage competition is Kür riding. Dressage, preeminently, is an art form. The Kür invites the rider to compose his own program, and thus elevates him from the rank of performing artist to that of creative artist. During a Kür ride the performer delights his spectators by his own composition. A musical analogy would be when Rachmaninoff played his own piano compositions. The rider is to compose an artistic program that is most suitable for expression by his instrument of art, his horse.

All dressage tests are compositions. But the standardized tests are created by others rather than those who ride it. Riding standard tests is performing art to which I personally prefer everyday dressage riding. For daily dressage work, indeed, is Kür riding. Never should daily riding be unplanned. Indeed, daily dressaging of the horse should be a composition in the rider's mind. Improvisations surely will be in order, embellishments surely necessary. But there will be freedom of expression, and the rider's imagination will be invited to take flight.

All serious dressage riders are riding Kürs in daily work. However, the Kür as a competition form remains a great challenge. The following reasons elevate the Kür, in my opinion, to the highest competition expression in riding:

1. The Kür offers a chance to become a composer as well as a performer of the composition of others. Emphasis is on logic of the gymnastic exercises, according to the innate possibilities of the horse, the instrument of expression.

2. Beauty will be expressed by a balanced use of all the horse's natural gaits, and in harmonious expression through transitions. Effortless elegance, unity of involvement, continuous, exhuberant movements,

and impeccable rhythm will make it almost a musical experience.

3. The composition will have to be made up of elements that are part of standardized dressage tests on any particular level on which the horse is ready to perform. Thus, for example, a rider may compose a Kür with the elements of the Prix de St. Georges, or the Grand Prix de Dressage standardized tests.

4. In a good Kür, as in any good composition of music, there must be balance in the structure. There should clearly be parts of introduction, text or statement, and a conclusion. The Kür should manifest a balanced ideology by showing off the horse, equally on both hands. Exercises should "mirror" each other, as an expression of the logic that the horse and rider have two equally important, and symmetrical sides.

5. Transitions should not only include those from one gait to another, but should include those within the paces, such as transitions from collected to extended trot.

6. There should be a balanced expression of both lateral and longitudinal bending gymnastics.

7. Display the strength of your instrument of art, the horse. Emphasize, if possible, his ability to do "extreme longitudinal transitions," such as a walk after extended trot, or departure in canter from a halt.

8. Think of the prescribed time limit. Be frugal with spaces. On long stretches show extended movements to save time. Fit your composition comfortably into the allotted time.

9. The brilliance of a Kür composition displays inventiveness in showing the best and ultimate knowledge of the horse within a confined space-time situation. Therein are the elements of art.

10. Try to ride your well-designed Kür to the accompaniment of music. Carefully select musical accompaniment to suit the exact timing of your paces. Tape recording allows the finest precision in coordinating musical selections to suit each movement. Films constantly involve this technique of perfectly timed musical accompaniment synchronized with visual action.

Usually competition Kürs are scored fifty percent on the horse's ability to correctly move through the exercises displayed. The other fifty percent of the score is awarded to the artistic merits of the composition itself. Thus the scores are equally balanced in rewarding the rider as a composer, and as the performer of his own composition. Obviously, the composition must be suitable to the ability and knowledge of the horse.

23
Why Is Jumping a
Dressage Activity?

There are many expressions in our language that are used in two or more connotations. Such is dressage. Another example would be the expression *classical* when referred to music or the fine arts. For instance *classical music* refers to all important music that has high artistic value, and therefore enduring appeal, as that is understood by experts. But there is a classical period within classical music that refers to a certain musical style, limited to one particular period in musical history. Exactly the same double meaning of the word *classical* is found in reference to the fine arts. All fine arts that have enduring artistic value are classical. But there is a particular classical style of art, limited to one particular epoch within the general mass of classical creations that shows enduring artistic value.

Dressage, in general, refers to any equestrian activity that is based on love and respect for the horse; equestrian activities that adhere to the classical principles of riding tradition, which are based on systematic development of the natural abilities of the horse to the greatest possible extent; equestrian activities that recognize that only through systematic, gradual, and correct gymnasticizing will the horse improve his natural abilities to their fullest possible extent. The inevitable result of correct dressaging is a mentally and physically obedient, supple, and balanced horse that is eager to move straight forward to the lightest aids.

The more limited meaning of the word *dressage* refers to the gymnastic exercises that will develop the abovementioned and desired balance, suppleness and obedience, while the horse's forward urge is not only preserved, but improved.

Obviously, jumping is part of dressage, when done correctly, according to the classical principles of riding. The life of a jumping horse is not spent over obstacles. A jumper is worked over fences less often than he is working on the flat ground. A jumper's life is mostly spent in gymnasticizing on the flat, and less frequently over fences. The jumper's gymnasticizing should differ in no way from the gymnasticizing of a horse whose activities are entirely devoted to dressage competitions.

All riders who jump know the attributes of an ideal jumper. Such a horse must be eager to move forward boldly; should be willing to respond to the slightest of aids, and respond to them promptly and correctly; should understand all the aids of legs, seat, and hands; should be obedient to his rider's commands; should be physically supple and mentally relaxed to negotiate with ease the most difficult fences; should work without mental resistance or physical stiffness, and with greatest conservation of his energies for purposes of jumping. His entire body should be mobilized, and his mind supremely concentrated; he should be able to bend longitudinally, and therefore change the length of his strides at ease for the slightest aids. He must be able to collect keenly and fly into extensions; all that without losing balance, and thus falling into the forehands rushing. He should obviously work on the reins on a light contact necessary for navigational support as well as fast and smooth steering. He should be laterally well bent for good curves and fast turns without any loss of impulsion. He should be able to carry the majority of the weight on his hindquarters; to carry as much as possible in the hindquarters for correct locomotion; to be able to crouch down on the hindquarters, to "coil all his springs" at the time of taking off. As a matter of fact, jumpers have to shift their weight so far back into the hindquarters as to enable them to lift their entire front off the ground at the time of take-off. A jumper taking off for a four-foot jump is much more seated than a Grand Prix de Dressage horse at the piaffe exercise.

Is there anything mentioned above not suitable to be expected of a good jumper? Is it not also dressage? Is it not identical to the goals of any dressage horse competing on the flat? Is it possible to create a jumper as described above without daily dressage work? No correctly jumping jumper can be created without dressage gymnastics.

There can be no meaningful work done over fences without doing it as part and parcel to dressage gymnastics. How could anyone do a simple exercise such as trotting over four Cavaletti ground poles without a relaxed, balanced, supple, and obedient horse? Is it not true that the horse must obey to stay in trot? Is he not to maintain his balance over the poles and continue evenly, without rushing, and arrow straight after the poles? Is he not to move on the rein in a light contact and responsive to the rider's legs and seat as these dictate him the length of strides and correct rhythm? Should he not be available for a halt soon after he passes over the poles? Should he not be able to bend into a curve to round the corner of the arena when he reaches it? Surely he has to do all that in spite of being schooled for jumping. Is it not true that a jumping course demands exactly the same attainments any dressage program demands of the horse? Is he not to do things predetermined at certain spots? Is he not to turn well and be handy? Is he not to move forward eagerly and without hesitation? Is he not to extend and collect his movements?

By now, I hope, it is apparent to the reader that jumping is also dressage—a branch of dressage, that, as dressage aims at developing the horse's potential to its utmost degree, dressage wishes to develop potential talented jumpers to be the greatest performers. Dressage very seldom, proportionately speaking, aims at the development of a horse for purely dressage purposes, for purposes of performing only in dressage competitions. Usually, in the majority of cases, through dressaging, a good jumper, a combined eventer, a hunter, or a pleasure horse is being created. In other words, dressage is a means to the attainment of several possible ends. In the past, of course, the majority of the horses trained through dressage were used as improved military campaign horses, and only a minority in the abovementioned sport horse categories.

Stadium Jumping

A stadium jumping course, at its best, resembles a cross-country jumping course, however, miniaturized. Indeed, stadium jumping courses developed out of the desire of spectators to oversee an entire jumping course comfortably from one spot. So a course of jumps was brought into a small area, and there, of necessity, the challenge was made artificial, and was formalized. Both horse and rider enjoy jumping in the open country, over natural obstacles that are connected by a course that is pleasant to follow, because of its natural beauty. In the confinement of a stadium course natural beauty more or less has vanished. It has been replaced by advertising billboards, spectators' stands, and electric wiring. Green grass, undulating hills have been ironed out to a table-flat sand arena. Natural, inviting, challenging obstacles have been replaced by vividly painted, artificially small, well-defined fences. The logical route leading across the country from one point of interest to another has been replaced by an artificially defined maze of loops and turns, confined to that sand pit, the arena.

Truly good stadium jumping courses stubbornly resemble the original cross-country jumping courses. The best of them are laid out on turf. The obstacles are as close to natural ones—such as one may have encountered a hundred years ago—as possible. They are built of birch branches, pine logs, unpainted pickets. They are embellished by green brush fences, or live, clipped shrubbery. The wings are hidden among live, planted pines, or graceful cedars. The take-off "bars" are natural flower beds in bloom, or clipped box hedges. The course is emerging in natural colors from a well-planted park. The ups and downs of the natural countryside may be replaced by banks, slides, mounds of dirt, in order to eliminate the boredom of a flat arena.

The Obstacle Course

Riders should walk the obstacle course before competing on it. Also, during training the jumping of a full course is called upon, riders must be asked to walk it. Good training always simulates the conditions and activities of competition. After all, the activities involved in competitions are standardized according to the highest levels of reasonableness. Therefore, that which is encouraged or required in competitions, is a reasonable and useful activity. It should be part of training activities, too. Without walking the competition or training course, a rider cannot plan his performance strategy. Riding a good course may be likened to the performance of a musical symphony or concerto. A jumping course is a composition. It does not consist of a number of individual jumps only. Similarly, a symphony is not made up of individual musical notes. Both are made up of a combination of all-important elements. The symphony is made up of moments of silences as important as those filled with sound. Similarly, the obtsacle course is made up of tracks of approach and departure just as important as the actual obstacles. A successful jump never occurs without the correct approach. The correct approach can never be created without the correct departure from the previous obstacle. As a matter of fact, when departures from and approaches to obstacles are correct, the fences are automatically cleared. Riders must perceive and then ride a course as a logical composition that has continuum.

Most horses refuse a jump or run out on a jump because they are brought there incorrectly. Either the line of approach, or the rhythm, or the level of collection, or all three, are incorrect before the horse will refuse an obstacle. When they do refuse because of the unreasonableness of their riders, they indeed save the rider's neck, for which the ungrateful rider usually beats them up. A horse who refuses a jump because he was brought there so as to make it impossible for him to negotiate it safely, should actually be rewarded by his rider.

As international jumping courses are built with as high and wide obstacles as a horse can possibly jump safely, the winners are determined by their ability to manipulate their horses between the jumps. The more balanced, supple, and obedient the horse is, the more likely he will win the competition. The good old days are gone with smallish obstacles were confronting talented jumpers on an easy line of approach. Now only those riders can consistently succeed in international jumping competitions who can determine the exact spot from which the horse will take flight over the jump. Moreover, they can determine at which level of collection the horse will be at that exact spot of stand-back to the jump. That presumes absolute control of both the horse's collection, and his rhythm and stride. All that presumes careful planning and strategy on the course. The rider, as he walks the course, must plan for each jump the ideal spot for takeoff, and the ideal level of "crouch" or collection of the horse for that take-off. Later, when riding, he must then be able to carry out his strategy.

No rider can do that sort of planning and that sort of riding when in the midst of competition. He must do it every time he jumps at home. He must be able to do it on ground Cavaletti poles at the trot. This kind of thing cannot be learned by a rider overnight. It emerges as a by-product of years of correct riding over Cavaletti exercises and combination jumps. It emerges as a by-product of consistent dressage gymnastics that both physically and mentally prepare a horse to carry out commands, and respond obediently to his rider's aids. It takes a well-gymnasticized, athletic horse with proper muscular strength, and well-developed joints. All these are the by-products of correct dressaging.

Since the most important things in a jumping competition happen on the flat between the jumps, the horse must be thoroughly dressaged to be able to bend longitudinally, in other words, collect and extend, while maintaining balance. Also, the horse is required to bend laterally, in other words bend through turns however small, and at a higher speed, without falling, losing balance and impulsion. Purity of rhythm is essential to jumping and that depends on the horse's balance on both straight and curved paths of progression. More than in pure dressage it is in jumping where a horse well flexed longitudinally and laterally will show superior results. In jumping the task is more difficult, indeed, than on the flat, for things happen faster, and when they don't happen the penalty is danger. Therefore a jumper, whether competing in stadium or cross-country, must be more gymnasticized, more able to flex, more able to bend, more obedient for safety reasons than any pure dressage horse that is competing on the flat and at a slower pace.

Jumping Training

Jumping training, as well as any other horse training, is very hard to write about. The success of daily training depends on practical assessment of a daily situation and creative genius to react to it in a novel way. Such things cannot be done in writing with a theoretical effort, limited to generalizations. Could written work do the training job, no instructors and coaches would be necessary in the art of riding.

In order to illuminate more, however, on how dressage is synonymous with correct jumping training, let me pursue the idea more specifically.

In equestrian art it is well to remember that not what you do, but how you do it, will determine the outcome. This is why it is so hard to write about it, for the nature of writing emphasizes the "what" over the "how." First of all, I wish to remind you once more that all horses worth working with in classical riding have, by virtue of their correct conformation, some jumping talents; that all horses, regardless how they will specialize later, must receive jumping training between the ages of four and six, for a two-year period of time. Without that, the correct development of joints, musculature, and rhythm will be impaired.

In general, work that will be demanded by the rider from the saddle, should be preceded by similar work done from the ground. Even in daily work, exercises on the longe tape, or from the hand, should precede exercises done from the saddle. But more important, before a certain thing is asked for by the rider in the saddle, the same thing should be introduced without the rider mounted. Thus, jumping should be introduced to the horse, at first, without a rider. Many fine breeding studs exercise their young horses, yearlings, by herding them cross-country. They make sure the terrain is not flat, and that it includes natural but easy obstacles. These herds of young horses are run through river beds, streams, ponds, over low logs, and many things they find challenging and fun in the environment. They go to pasture, and return for the night, through these obstacles.

Much later, when we begin to work our fine, well-bred, and well-founded three year old, we must continue to free-jump him. Any good riding establishment should have a free-jumping run. It is vastly important, in order to avoid damage to the legs, to have very low jumps placed in this run. Little logs, narrow, dry ditches, or some with water, clipped shrubs, and the like, will serve the purpose. None should be higher than two feet, and about that wide also. The horse should be released at one end of the run, and urged to run the length of it boldly, negotiating the little jumps. On the other end he should be awaited by a friendly person with awards, including sugar, carrots, and apples. After awards, the horse should be sent back on the run. This, depending on the length of training, should be repeated a certain number of times daily. After this exercise the horse can be saddled and ridden in dressage gymnastics appropriate for his age and training level.

Four-year-old horses, well prepared by gymnastics on the flat, can begin to jump under the rider. Preliminary to mounting, on jumping days, the horse should still be working over fences, free of saddle and rider. Now the fences can be as high as four feet, and combinations should be included.

Jumping on the longe line is not harmful, but inferior as an exercise to free-jumping in a run. The horse is rather acutely bent on a longe line, and his impulsion may be restricted. He has a chance to evade by running out. But if he is jumped on the longe he ought to move over low poles, not higher than two feet, and over a maximum of only two such poles. These should be placed opposite each other on the arc of the circle. Valuable natural jumps, unfortunately, must be excluded. Bold, forward impulsion will be compromised. The value of muscle development, timing rhythm, and courage will be diminished on the longe, in comparison with a straight run. It is best to teach horses to manipulate bending courses from the saddle. Free-jumping should be on straight runs, and done rather boldly. Therein is its value.

From the saddle, serious jumping training begins when the horse is four years old. For one year he has been working under the saddle and is supple enough, strong enough, and obedient enough to the aid to receive jumping instruction.

At the beginning all jumping instruction should be based on Cavaletti work. Later combination fences are added. These two elements of jumping training should persistently stay as the major part of exercises throughout the career of the jumper. Therefore comments on Cavaletti work and gymnastics on combination fences are important.

There is a sufficient amount and some especially excellent literature on jumping in general, and Cavaletti work in particular. However, in this space, let me make some simple generalizations about them.

At the beginning of the horse's training (later when he is a knowledgeable jumper at the beginning of his daily work over fences) always build all Cavaletti and combination jumps at correctly measured distances. The correctness of these distances will always be determined by your horse's conformation and his level of athletic development. You will know these distances by simply observing where his feet print on the ground when moving in the pace you want to use during these exercises.

Later in advanced training, and then only after working over "correctly" distanced combinations, introduce irregular or odd distances between your fences, in order to check how successfully you can control the horse's work over them. In international competitions most combinations are "out of stride" to make sure that only riders with enough control and strategy can successfully negotiate them. On lesser competitions you will find that most combinations will be "off stride" because you will seldom ride the "average horse" (usually nonexistent) to whose stride the combination will be adjusted in order to suit the potpourri of conformations competing. However, over smaller fences distances matter less, because your horse can clear them with a larger stand-back, or "bunny hop" them if necessary.

A good rider, however, even on a low course, will insist on strategic riding, that being his chance to practice it, and will insist on demanding that his horse take off in rhythm when so aided in order to reaffirm obedience and correct control.

Right at the beginning of jumping training, ideally, the horse should be ridden over open country twice a week, and worked over Cavaletti poles twice a week at the trot. On other days work should continue by dressage gymnastics on the flat. When quiet, controlled negotiation of cross-country terrains and small obstacles is achieved, and the horse is trotting with pure rhythm over Cavaletti poles, other things may be introduced.

Now combinations should be jumped. Always approach them from the trot, possibly through trot Cavaletti poles. Once having leaped into the combination, maintain the canter strides through them. Make those units of Cavaletti fences that are being jumped rather than trotted over as varied in looks as possible: some vertical, some spread; some natural colored, some brightly painted. Some should involve ditches.

During these increasingly sophisticated Cavaletti exercises add a variety of distances, always correctly measured, to call for a different number of strides from fence to fence. Include every day some fences between which there is absolutely no stride, and thus demand rhythmic hopping. Toward the end of your daily session introduce the maximum height you planned to clear on that day.

Later, when you can be sure of the horse's development in observation, courage, cadence, and rhythm, in addition to calm obedience, strength, suppleness, and good balance, introduce some single fences. Trot to them as often as possible. Every jump made from trot is worth gold in developing correct use of the horse's body over fences, which is indicated by the "bascule." He learns best to navigate in flight also when he takes off from the trot. Not speed should catapult him into flight, but rather a correctly developed musculature, propelled by knowledge-able use of it. Depending on the horse's jumping talent, you can trot to relatively high fences. As an average, four-foot-high obstacles can still be negotiated from a trot.

When jumping height, to check how well the horse has developed his ability to clear high fences, elevate the obstacle gradually. Jump height always as part of a combination, and with correctly measured distance between the "adjustive," low, first pole and the obstacle of elevation that should be the last unit.

Communication

Communication is not only constant, but is also both ways, going on between horse and rider. Riding is a dialogue. Riders who lack the sensitivity, and do not actively cultivate the sensitivity of perceiving the horse's "aids," will never be superb equestrian artists. The medium of equestrian art is alive. He must participate willingly in the creation of the artistic impression. He must consent to that effort and lend himself to the will of the rider. In an age like ours most people must make a conscious effort to treat living things with the insight and respect they deserve. There is a distinct tendency to treat living things, including people, as if they were gadgets. A horse is alive, and equestrian art, in other words classical riding, serves his ends, not the ego of the rider.

The negative, uncooperative efforts of the horse are always invited by ample causes. Causes may originate with the rider, or may be a re-sult of the horse's weaknesses. Never forget that when the horse does not perform successfully that which is asked of him, he has sufficient reasons for refusing to do so. There is always a hierarchy of uncoopera-tion. First, the horse communicates tension. Then he develops resistance. Finally, he will disobey the rider. A sensitive equestrian will respond already to tension, thereby preventing the occurrence of resistance and of disobedience. Good care must be taken that disobedience be avoided at all cost, for the horse succeeding in disobeying will remember that he is ultimately sovereign, that the rider is his victim. That lesson should never be taught! For the essence of classical riding, of artistic riding, is that the medium of the art form, the horse, be the obedient subject in the hand of the master, the rider. Submission must occur by respectful cooperation of the horse. It must never be extracted by fear.

On the following table I will suggest the proper rider reactions to the horse's communications of uncooperativeness:

The Rider's Possible Responses to the Horse's Initiatives

HORSE communicates		RIDER properly responds
1) Tension	(followed by)	Prevention by relaxation
2) Resistance	" "	Correction and corrective exercises
3) Disobedience	" "	Punishment

Let us examine in more detail the meaning of the table.

Tension develops when the horse feels uncomfortable about something. It may be physical stress that is resultant from overdemanding. It may be mental anguish, usually fear of something. It is well to know, to detect, the cause of tension that the horse communicates. For depending on its cause we must select the proper methods of preventing its intensification into resistance. If the cause is physical stress, due to fatigue of muscles or joints, our diminishing demands will relax the horse. He should get some rest on a long rein, or exercising should continue with easier, more basic movements that he can perform with comfort. He can be reassured with patting and stroking. We must reduce our demands on his physique. We must proceed more cautiously with our gymnastic goals.

If the horse became tense due to mental anguish, usually fear, we must reassure him that the object of fear is really not threatening. We must show him the object he fears, let him face it, and approach it on his own accord. We must merely encourage him to approach the feared object by insisting on him facing it but without forcing him to advance toward it.

Horses are curious, and will approach all objects voluntarily, regardless of how much they fear it, provided the rider shows no fear of it and is willing to wait. After all, a well-dressaged horse ultimately trusts, and therefore obeys, his rider's decisions. The rider, therefore, must keep the horse facing the object of fear. He must use his seat and legs in mild urging toward the object. Every step the horse takes toward it must be instantly rewarded by petting and a relaxation of leg and seat aids. It may take time, but we have the means to convince our horse that there is nothing to be feared of the strange object he resented.

Thus, physical or mental tension should be reduced by the rider diminishing his demands, or showing reassured courage, respectively.

Resistance occurs only after tension has been allowed to accumulate without taking notice of it, or by neglecting to reduce it. When a horse resents our demands, we must renew our strategy. We must either pretend that we wanted less than what he understood, or continue exercising by repetition for shorter periods of time. As resistance develops from tension, obviously it can also be of either physical or mental origin.

Disobedience by the horse is usually well deserved by the rider. If the rider is insensitive enough to take no notice of tension and resistance in the horse, he will have to cope with disobedience.

Often disobedience occurs when the horse is a better judge of a situation than the rider. If such is the case, the rider should reward his horse for disobedience.

The following example comes readily to mind: Once, in California, during a three-day-event competition a rider on cross-country course felt tension, then resistance in his horse. The trail was narrow, the competition keen, time important, so the rider forcefully pushed on. The horse disobeyed this increased and forceful demand, reared spun around on the narrow trail, and was ready to reverse his course. Then, looking back, the rider noticed a rattlesnake uncoil and slither away from the path. This disobedience must be rewarded. The horse's instinct, attentiveness, independent judgment under these circumstances were commendable and admirable.

More commonly one sees a tense, than resistant horse forced toward a demanding obstacle. Due to the rider's interference he may arrive at the difficult obstacle unprepared by training, and hindered by current rider activities. He simply cannot take off and clear the jump. He could merely land on top of it. He disobeys the command to jump, thereby saving his and his rider's life. As undesirable as it is to be eliminated from competition, so it is desirable to stay alive and be without broken bones. The horse is obviously a wiser judge of the situation than his foolish rider who overdemanded of him.

In most cases, however, disobedience should be punished. the horse must willingly submit to the commands of the rider. He must learn that there is no room for compromise, especially when the rider's demands are reasonable. Punishment should seldom be by the whip. There are many other, wiser means of punishment. It is well that the whip remains regarded by the horse as an aid, rather than as a source of painful punishment.

For instance, when an advanced horse disobeys by bolting away, an obvious attempt at temporary vacation from the rider's control, he could be instantly halted, kept halted for a few minutes to show the rider's supreme command, and that when he disobeys by rushing, he must yield to its opposite: total immobility. Or a horse may, for example, disobey an aid to move forward with good impulsion. Let us say, he will not canter away from a walk. He should be punished by making him extend his trot. He must be made to go forward, the very thing he refused to do, not in the contested mode, however, i.e., canter, but in another mode, the trot.

When there is no other reasonable way to punish but by wielding the crop, do it instantly upon disobedience. The horse cannot connect punishment with any event a minute later. Again, remember, a good equestrian thinks and feels like a horse, not like a human. We can be punished for misdeeds effectively months later, after having been told what the punishment is for. Not horses. With them the whip must crack instantly. It is important to know also that one single, strong crack of the whip does all. Prolonged beating is useless, cruel, unreasonable. One strong sting on the horse's side, right behind the rider's leg, does the whole job. Should you desire to go on for a prolonged thrashing, you must know that then you have a problem, not your horse.

24
The Meaning of Dressage

Dressage, this French term with no proper English equivalent, mystifies many people and, as most mysteries, antagonizes some. When inquiring about any specific subject matter or academic discipline, we must accept the usage of specific *terminus technicus* or technical terminology. Instead of shrinking from such terminology we should derive pleasure from its acquisition. The more one acquires expertise in an area of knowledge, the more one becomes familiar with the concepts related to that knowledge. The more detailed and sophisticated our knowledge becomes the more we must rely on specific terminology, denoting exactly what we mean. For us, in California, it is sufficient to know the word *snow*, for we can afford to be semiignorant regarding it. However, our primitivity concerning snow will not suffice in the Arctic regions, where Eskimos are known to use two dozen specific words denoting different conditions of snow.

Likewise, for any person ignorant concerning horses the word *riding* suffices conversationally, *riding* meaning any situation when a human being is sitting on top of a horse. Such general conceptualization, however, will not suffice for the ambitious student of equestrian sports.

So let me introduce some meaning to the technical term *dressage*. The term is used in three different connotations:

1. *Dressage*, in general, refers to all riding that adheres to the classical riding traditions. These traditions have their roots in the writings of Xenophon, who lived more than two thousand years ago. Since his introduction of the classical principles of horsemanship, centuries of evolution helped crystallize, focus, refine, and define classical riding. All has been tried. Some succeeded. That which succeeded did so because it produced the best and most lasting results with horses. Success, practical results, were consistently produced by a certain mode of

horsemanship. That successful, pragmatic horsemanship is synonymous with classical horsemanship. It is, for short, called *dressage*.

2. *Dressage* is used also with a slightly different connotation. It denotes the purposeful, logical gymnasticizing of a horse. When purposefully riding through useful, logical exercises, the rider is doing dressage.

3. *Dressage* often means specific competition events. When used to denote such competitions, then dressage riding simply means the sequential, predetermined showing of specific gymnastic exercises.

Then in short there are these three meanings to the word *dressage*:

1. Dressage is all riding based on the two thousand years of classical riding experience and its resultant successes.

2. Dressage is all the natural gymanstics performed by the horse for the improvement of his natural abilities.

3. Dressage is any exhibition, mostly in competition, that shows the accomplishments of a naturally developed athletic horse, mostly by riding a prescribed program of exercises.

Everybody rides dressage who is riding according to the following classical principles, even if he never heard the word *dressage*.

The *Attitude* of the classical rider is determined by his love and respect for the horse. Therefore (1) He desires to develop only the horse's natural abilities, for the sake of the horse, to their highest possible degree, thereby fulfilling the horse's inborn destiny by unfolding his native talents. This will result in a happy, healthy, long-living horse who has been awakened to the fullest realization of his intelligence, and has accomplished much with a minimum of stress. (2) He will develop the horse's natural abilities through patience, thereby gaining the sympathetic cooperation of his horse. He will improve his horse through the methods well known in the best of human education, without force, without incurring fear, and without artificial means. He will enjoy the process of education as much as its brilliant manifestations in correct achievements. (3) He will attempt to penetrate the nature of his horse, and as much as possible will perpetually monitor his needs, thinking and feeling and acting according to those dictates.

The *result* of classical horsemanship will be the following: (1) A horse that moves straight forward with zest; who will be moving in rhythm, with clarity in all natural paces, and in balance. He will invite his rider to merge with him in harmonious motion. He will allow his rider to control his movements, and direct his energies. He will move rhythmically and supply, and will yield to subtle aids obediently. (2) A horse who will be improved physically, athletically; who will use his entire body for carrying his rider; who will be aware of his body, and will use it properly for the performance of various tasks. (3) A horse who will be mentally obedient, for he has learned to trust the judgment and commands of his rider; who has grown to understand human communication and the language of aids; who can relax in the company of his rider and render himself at his disposal.

The horse's physical and mental development is: simultaneous; reinforce one another; is achieved by systematic, consistent, and logical gymnastic exercises.

The systematic, consistent, and logical gymnasticizing of a horse is also called *dressage*, as mentioned above. These exercises are designed to increase the horse's ability to bend *longitudinally* and *laterally*.